Religious power assumes many strikingly different forms, which are often regarded both by believers and by students of religion as unique, unrelated, and even mutually exclusive. In this book, however, I. M. Lewis adopts a holistic approach and argues that to understand the nature of spiritual power we need to appreciate how these apparently contradictory mystical manifestations are in fact part of a single complex of mutually defining and sustaining elements. Stressing the importance of rigorous social contextualization, he analyzes such seemingly disparate phenomena as spirit-possession, witchcraft, cannibalism, and shamanism, which are usually attributed to separate cults and even cultures, revealing the interconnections both between them and with the world religions, such as Islam and Christianity. This expanded and revised edition includes two new chapters, taking spider symbolism in the Italian tarantist spirit cult as a point of departure for a radical critique of Mary Douglas's theory of dangerous anomalies; and showing how the exorcism of spirits in Buddhism, Christianity, and Islam serves to entrench the power of men over women.

Besides presenting a critique of the treatment of religious phenomena as reified, Professor Lewis demonstrates – in an intriguing deconstruction of the classic anthropological fieldwork situation that he sees as itself a kind of shamanic initiation – the complexity of the problem of understanding other peoples' beliefs, and the way in which these beliefs often inadvertently become part of anthropological theory. He emphasizes the continuing strength in social and cultural anthropology of a comparative approach that constantly seeks to force anthropological "theory" into a dialogue with ethnographic particulars, thereby encouraging the distillation of empirically more satisfactory theory.

This illumination of critical aspects of religious power, a demonstration of the value of a comparative approach in the formulation of anthropological theory, will interest scholars and students of social and cultural anthropology and religious studies, as well as other readers concerned with the nature of religion in the modern world.

RELIGION IN CONTEXT

RELIGION IN CONTEXT

Cults and charisma

I. M. LEWIS

London School of Economics and Political Science

Second edition

CAMBRIDGE
UNIVERSITY PRESS

Published by the Press Syndicate of the University of Cambridge
The Pitt Building, Trumpington Street, Cambridge CB2 1RP
40 West 20th Street, New York, NY 10011–4211, USA
10 Stamford Road, Oakleigh, Melbourne 3166, Australia

First published 1986
Reprinted 1987, 1988, 1989
Second edition 1996

Printed in Great Britain at the University Press, Cambridge

A catalogue record for this book is available from the British Library

Library of Congress cataloguing in publication data
Lewis, I. M.
Religion in context: cults and charisma / I. M. Lewis. – 2nd ed.
p.   cm.
Includes bibliographical references and index.
ISBN 0 521 56234 1. – ISBN 0 521 56634 7 (pbk.)
1. Cults. 2. Religions. 3 Witchcraft. 4. Cannibalism.
5. Shamanism. 6. Anthropology. I. Title.
BL80.2.L48 1996
291–dc20   95–20517 CIP

ISBN 0 521 56234 1 hardback
ISBN 0 521 56634 7 paperback

WD

Contents

Preface

The beliefs and behavior conventionally distinguished as "witch-craft," "spirit-possession," "cannibalism," and "shamanism" seem at first sight to have little in common. Anthropologists and other students of comparative religion regularly treat these phenomena as totally unrelated and even mutually exclusive, objectified "things" characteristic of different cults and of distinctive types (and stages) of culture and society. This book takes a different view. It argues that, on the contrary, these are actually closely related expressions of mystical power, or "charisma." In fact, as we shall see when we examine them closely, each illuminates the others, and the integrative, comparative approach advocated here enables us to understand how the conquest and transformation of malign forces ("negative charisma") empowers the leaders of charismatic cults, whose status is always potentially ambiguous. Especially where they occupy a marginal position in relation to a world religion, such cults of affliction are frequently stigma-tized in their wider social context as "superstitious survivals." Our analysis indicates that, on the contrary, such cults are often recent developments which, with the attribution of the unorthodox to the past, actually play a crucial role in the definition of orthodox belief itself.

In endeavoring to elucidate these contrasting configura-tions of mystical power by emphasizing their underlying interconnections rather than their differences, I also seek to display the continuing value in social (and cultural) anthro-pology of a comparative analysis – one that continually seeks to force anthropological "theory" into a dialogue with

ix

ethnographic "facts," encouraging the distillation of empirically more satisfactory theory. This empiricist dialogue is
indeed complex, as I emphasize in the opening chapter, which
reflects upon anthropological fieldwork itself as a form of
shamanistic initiation. Questioning the glib anthropological
construction of culturally representative "cosmologies,"
Chapter 1 explores the origins of "anthropological" theories of
witchcraft and their relation to native beliefs and disbeliefs.
The standard psycho-dynamic, social-tension theory of
witchcraft as an expression of jealousy and spite is, as we see
borrowed directly from the native sources to which it is applied
by anthropologists. This in turn offers an illuminating
epidemiological perspective for understanding the incidence
of those afflictions affecting particularly women, which are
interpreted in terms of spirit-possession and which involve
spirits that indirectly exert pressure on the opposite sex.
Hence the anthropological theory of witchcraft, derived from
ethnographic sources, also helps us to understand and analyze
the ethnography of spirit-possession.

In the same comparativist vein, Chapter 2 explores another
aspect of spirit possession – its animal symbolism in the case
of the Italian tarantist cult of the tarantula spider-spirit
which, it is argued, provides a novel point of departure for a
critique of Mary Douglas's classic theory of animal "anomalies." These, as we shall see, turn out to be very ambiguously
grounded in the "ethnographic facts" of the Lele people of the
Congo, whose animal categories are the source of Douglas's
theory which centers on the "anomalous" nature of the scaly
ant-eater, or pangolin. The Lele environment, in fact, includes
several distinct types of pangolin which evoke different Lele
responses in ways that cast serious doubt on the validity of
Douglas's interpretation. The situation becomes even more
complex when we take account of the variability in the treatment by neighboring ethnic groups of the different pangolins
of the Congo region.

This problem, which Douglas's theory does not address,
suggests new hypotheses which look to cosmological differences to explain the variable treatment of pangolin species as

potential spirit animals. More generally, as our comparison of spider and pangolin symbolism is intended to highlight, where two or more related natural species are subject to differential religious treatment, a satisfactory interpretation should explain why one is selected for preferential attention. The pangolin case, however, cannot really be fully elucidated on the basis of the existing ethnographic evidence. We need new comparative research on the symbolic treatment of the pangolin as a sacred or spirit animal.

In Chapter 3 we explore the epidemiology of spirit possession, tracing the implications of the vulnerability which we find women display to spirit attack. Here women are in effect marginalized by men and develop cults which, in relation to male religion, are also marginal and typically involve "peripheral" spirits that are foreign to local mainstream culture. Of course, this is not necessarily how women themselves see their situation, nor is it in any sense an "objective" assessment of the actual importance of women in a given society. I emphasize this because, although it seems fairly obvious, my argument has often been misunderstood here.

Since possession of this kind is something for which, in the societies where it occurs, women can hardly be blamed, there are here intriguing analogies to that recalcitrant case in witchcraft studies – the self-confessing, involuntary witch. Such "introvert" self-accusing witches, who often turn out to be women desperately seeking help, like their spirit-possessed counterparts, are in effect mystically licensed to exert pressure on their immediate circle. Thus, through applying the theory of witchcraft analysis to spirit-possession, we reap the additional reward of gaining new insights into the dynamics of witchcraft itself.

This prompts the general reconsideration we embark upon in Chapter 4 of types of witchcraft (and sorcery) as modes of mystical attack, suggesting that, in their effects, spirit-possession and "introspective" witchcraft are milder forms of mystical aggression, employed against superiors, than are "extrovert" accusations against inferiors. A limiting factor here, apparently, is that the charismatic leaders of possession cults risk being charged with witchcraft and denounced as witches.

This anthropological understanding of the dynamics of witchcraft and spirit-possession is informed by the generally disbelieving stance of the anthropologist. This has had, as we see in Chapter 5, a curious effect on anthropological studies of cannibalism, where reports of cannibalism in witchcraft contexts have been dismissed as fantasy while often being uncritically accepted in non-witchcraft contexts! Here the cannibalistic reputation acquired by Europeans in colonial Africa after their suppression of witchcraft (and, hence, inadvertent protection of witches) should give us pause. A more enlightening approach to the meaning of cannibalism as ideology or practice acknowledges this relationship with witchcraft and takes the analysis of mystical power one stage farther, stressing its connection with various modes of sexual aggression.

Although, as I emphasize, it is never unambiguously so, in all these contexts mystical power is seen primarily as a negative force. The dramatic conquest of this malign power is, as Chapter 6 insists, the archetypal foundation for the assumption of the charismatic role par excellence – that of the shaman. This is the most positive meaning placed upon affliction as the basis for initiation into charismatic cults. As soon as the treatment takes the form of domestication rather than exorcism, it becomes a charismatic initiation rite of the type central to shamanism. As I argue, misleading reifications that treat "positive" and "negative" mystical experience separately have prevented anthropologists and others from appreciating the ubiquitous character of shamanistic initiation and its position in the "career structure" of spirit-possession cults. Ethnographic data again force us to revise anthropological theory.

Naturally, the domestication (adorcism) of spirits in the course of the development of the shamanic career, or more temporarily as a treatment for a specific affliction, is not the only option. Exorcism, which is the principal other possible response has, Chapter 7 argues, its own modalities, linking it with gender and male power. Theoretically, accommodation (adorcism) and exorcism would seem equally appropriate responses to sickness and affliction attributed to spirit possession. But, when we look carefully at how each of these alternative treatments is actually mobilized in male-dominated Christian, Muslim, and Buddhist cultures, we find that exorcism is the treatment preferred by men in contrast to women's preference for adorcism. Exorcism thus, generally, seems to serve the interests of male hierarchy – but, as we shall see, does not always engender a contrasting reaction in the form of a women's cult, based on adorcism. In fact, exorcism turns out in practise to be a more complex and problematic process than at first appears. It proves difficult to be definitively rid of troublesome spirits, or for the exorcist to avoid what amounts to contamination by the expelled spirits.

As well as providing a better understanding of the internal dynamics of charismatic cults, this cumulative comparative analysis also highlights the external role of marginal cults in the broader definition of ideological boundaries. My final chapter shows (with reference to African Islam) how these marginal, local cults are classified officially (against the historical evidence) as "survivals" and so contribute to the dynamic process of adjustment by which universal world religions define and redefine metropolitan orthodoxy by contrasting it to "primitive superstition." The price centrality pays to marginality for providing this service is, in effect, the ambiguous power it cedes to the latter. This dialectical context forces us to scrutinize carefully the concept of "survival" and prompts at the same time a better understanding of the nature and needs of orthodoxy. It also takes our analysis of the precipitating circumstances of women's peripheral spirit-possession a stage further, showing how the extent of the involvement of wives in these cults may become an index of *embourgeoisement* and male respectability and so become linked to the changing status of women. And here, for the moment at any rate, I rest my case. At least I hope to have demonstrated the advantages of this general comparative approach to configurations of mystical energy that are usually reified and treated as though they had no connection with one another – and so are, as I argue, gravely misunderstood.

This volume, as I must remind the reader in conclusion, is also intended as a demonstration of the enduring validity in social anthropology (here in the anthropological study of religion), of an empiricist methodology which, in the elucidation of social forces and formations, commits data and theory to an on-going, creative dialogue. Needless to say, this approach rejects the self-indulgent and ultimately stultifying vogue of 1970s and 1980s anthropology for "post-modernist," "reflective," and "literary" (a term used rather optimistically!) modes of discourse, where, since everything in ethnographic rendering is deemed to be equally valid, literally anything goes.

Chapters 1 and 3, based on formal public lectures, have been left essentially in the form in which they were originally delivered, issues raised by Chapter 3 and subsequent developments being elaborated in the following chapters. In revising this latter material particularly, I have benefited from discussions with a wide range of colleagues and friends at the universities of Budapest, Helsinki, Illinois, Indiana, Kyoto, Naples, Osaka, Pennsylvania, Rome, Urbino, and Washington (to mention only the more distant). As usual, I am especially grateful to Joan Wells, Caroline Simpson, and Carol Evans for typing (and retyping) so much of this book. Christina Toren's help in systematizing and checking the notes and bibliography is also warmly appreciated. I wish, finally, to thank Roger Smedley for revising and improving the index.

Acknowledgments

Chapter 1 is based on an inaugural lecture, "The anthropologist's muse," delivered at the London School of Economics on October 17, 1973.

Chapter 2 was originally published as "The spider and the pangolin" in *Man* 26, no. 3 (1991): 513–25.

Chapter 3 is an edited version of the Malinowski Memorial Lecture for 1966, originally published in *Man* 1, no. 3 (1966): 307–25.

Chapter 4 is a revised version of "A Structural Approach to Witchcraft and Spirit Possession," originally published in M. Douglas (ed.), *Witchcraft Confessions and Accusations* (London, Tavistock, 1970), pp. 293–310.

Chapter 5 is an expanded version of a lecture given at the Laboratoire Peiresc (Valbonne) and at the Universities of Urbino and Kyoto, and printed in abbreviated form in *Research: Contributions to Interdisciplinary Anthropology* 2 (1983): 39–50.

Chapter 6 is an extended version of a paper, "What is a Shaman?," originally published in *Folk* 23 (1981): 25–36.

Chapter 7 was first published as "Exorcism and male control of religious experience" in *Ethnos* 1–2 (1990): 26–40.

Chapter 8 developed from a lecture first given at Accademia dei Lincei (Rome, 1981) and later published in *Temenos* 19 (1983): 55–67.

The author thanks the editors of these publications for permission to reprint this material in its revised form here.

CHAPTER I

Anthropological fieldwork
and the context of belief

I

Those who are not social or cultural anthropologists must be surprised at the deep metaphysical significance we attach to fieldwork in exotic settings as a necessary condition in our formation and continued existence as practicing anthropologists. Malinowski's patron and the first regular teacher of our subject at the London School of Economics, Professor C. G. Seligman, did not exaggerate when he eloquently pleaded for research funds with the words "Field research in anthropology is what the blood of the martyrs is to the Church."[1] If only the one had flowed as freely as the other! It makes us what we are: Without it we are nothing. So, if you ask most students why they want to study anthropology, you will be told disarmingly, "To do fieldwork." And if you are so ill-advised as to attend a staff meeting in any university anthropology department, you will be amazed at the rancorous clamor that breaks out as soon as we reach that perennial agenda item, our competing claims to apply for leave to carry out further research overseas.

Fieldwork thus is our Utopia, our millennial dream. In such an atmosphere mere "library research," as it is disparagingly described, is virtually taboo – a possibility, perhaps for lame ducks and rainy days. The ultimate test of the professional anthropologist's standing remains the successful completion of a major piece of field research in exotic surroundings. It is necessary also for the researcher to display an impressive command of the relevant vernacular and present the results of his heroic endeavors in an appropriately detailed and scholarly monograph where they can be carefully scrutinized. The more difficult, dangerous, and inaccessible the terrain, the better. Similarly, the longer the period of fieldwork, the greater the student's merit. So the number of years and months (and sometimes even weeks) notched up under the sun is studiously logged and scrutinized by our recording angels. These statistics are carefully preserved and figure prominently in that fascinating ethnographic document, *The Register of Members of the Association of Social Anthropologists of the Commonwealth*.[2]

In this tradition, the most damaging criticism that can be lodged against a colleague concerns the quality of his fieldwork. Did he *really* get the facts right? Did he *really* speak the local language with sufficient proficiency for us to accept his complicated interpretation of their symbols? Do his findings represent a view biased by his close association with only one section of the community he studied? Suspicions of this sort dog the reputations, and sometimes threaten the careers, of even the most dazzling theoreticians if they have not also given acceptable proof of their scholarship as fieldworkers. Here Lévi-Strauss's case is particularly interesting. As he himself sometimes admits and as his warmest British advocates acknowledge,[3] his field research is patchy and thin and falls far short of the standards Malinowski established. Indeed, most of his theoretical writing relies heavily on information collected by other anthropologists and is in this sense markedly dependent on secondary sources. Yet he proclaims the crucial role of fieldwork for our subject and exhibits highly ambivalent attitudes toward it. Replying to a spirited attack by the French sociologist Gurvitch, Lévi-Strauss accuses the latter of misunderstanding and exaggerating the aims of anthropology. We do not, he retorts loftily, attempt to reach as complete a knowledge as possible of the societies we study. And he continues, "The disparity between such an ambition and the resources available to us is so great that we might be called charlatans, and with good reason. How would one penetrate the dynamics of an alien society after a stay of a few months, knowing nothing of its history, and usually very little of its language?"[4]

This interesting riposte, to which it is tempting to rejoin, "Speak for yourself," contrasts sharply with another passage by the same author. Here, again in reply to Gurvitch, Lévi-Strauss parades by name the various ethnic groups he has visited in South America and protests indignantly, "All these names are associated with men and women of whom I have been fond, whom I have respected, whose faces remain in my memory. They remind me of joys, hardships, weariness and, sometimes, dangers. *These are my witness* [emphasis supplied], the living link between my theoretical views and reality."[5] And in a later passage, he announces even more insistently, perhaps even defiantly, "I am an anthropologist who has conducted fieldwork."[6] This is not the image of Lévi-Strauss with which we are most familiar, but it is one of the many facets of his intriguing situation to which I shall return later. We may also note here how one of the currently most influential schools of American anthropology makes a similar and more direct fetish of fieldwork through its slogan, "New Ethnography." By this title it seeks to appropriate the prestige that traditionally attaches to the most minutely detailed and scrupulous collection of field data.

As further evidence of the anthropologist's obsession with fieldwork in alien cultures, the peculiar position of the anthropologist who investigates his own culture merits attention. As one would expect, orthodox opinion holds that such research is of dubious legitimacy. The distance between the observer and the observed is not considered sufficiently wide to generate those sparks of intercultural inspiration so essential to the anthropological imagination. Yet is this always and necessarily so? Few societies are truly homogeneous. Most contain significant and to some degree mutually incomprehensible cultural distinctions. This is one reason why it is perfectly possible for a British patrial to carry out authentic anthropological research in the United Kingdom. Ulster is perhaps a rather extreme example of such a setting. There is also the consideration that the autochthonous anthropologist in a sense often does his fieldwork in reverse. The imaginative leaps in such cases occur not so much in the actual collection of ethnographic data as in the analysis and writing-up.

Finally, if fieldwork is crucial in our subject, different methods of doing it should produce different kinds of anthropology. In a sense, this has always been a dominant assumption, one that underlies the great importance we all attach to Malinowski's influence. In this vein, Audrey Richards[7] has pointed out how the contrasting characteristics of French and British anthropology reflect their different modes of fieldwork. The light-footed French descend in droves like locusts upon their terrain, making a succession of short, sharp probes. These may be continued at intervals over a decade or more and sometimes culminate in a sudden final climactic confrontation when the peoples they study at last submit to this relentless goading and expose their hidden souls. How different we British anthropologists are! Our approach is solitary, more intensive and concentrated as we doggedly attempt to unravel and record for posterity the dominant features of a whole culture in eighteen to twenty-four months of uninterrupted work and total immersion in the world of our hosts. We share the same Muse as our French colleagues, but we practice her rites in a different style.

Through this romantic quest for knowledge and illumination from the uncharted peoples of the Third World – those for the most part traditionally neglected by more conventional European scholarship – social anthropology can legitimately claim to stand as the authentic founder of black studies, the original academic discipline devoted to the study of alternative cultures, institutions, and beliefs. We are thus true transcultural transvestites, professional aliens, cross-cultural voyeurs. And fieldwork is primarily a matter of observation and detection, so that abundant natural curiosity is an essential attribute of the successful research worker. Whether he likes it or not, every anthropologist is in practice a private eye, prying relentlessly and often irritatingly into the affairs of his foreign hosts and so intruding savagely on their privacy. No wonder most anthropologists, whatever their intentions,

political opinions, or connections, are regarded at some stage
in fieldwork as spies. (There is a curious harmony between this
sinister aspect of the most empirical part of anthropology and
the current fashion that terms such as "hidden messages,"
"codes" to be "cracked," and other jargon borrowings from the
communications industry enjoy in that rarefied world of
symbolic analysis known to its intimates, a little unfortunately
perhaps, as semiology.) Such indeed is the field-worker's
privileged intimacy with his informants that, if we are to
follow some authorities, it automatically rules out marriage as
well as other, less formal romantic attachments. So, according
to Margaret Mead, one of the particular hazards likely to arise
in studying what she somewhat old-fashionedly calls "high
cultures" is the danger that the anthropologist might actually
want to marry his or her informants![8]

II

Fieldwork is for us also a voyage in a different sense, since it is
the royal road to the anthropological calling. The would-be
anthropologist trains for fieldwork, disappears into the field,
and finally returns to write up the research, collect a Ph.D.,
and embark upon a professional career. As a number of
anthropologists have noticed, and none more perceptively
than Rosemary Firth,[9] we see here the familiar tripartite
structure common to most transition rituals. In the first
phase, the neophyte prepares to surrender his old status and
to shed ethnocentric assumptions. In the second, "liminal"
phase, he retires to learn the new culture of his hosts. In the
third phase, he reemerges to be readopted within his own
academic culture in a new role as professional anthropologist.
Each stage has its attendant traumas, which have to a certain
extent become conventionalized, the most taxing being those
of the actual field research and subsequent writing-up. Here,
however, there is a deep paradox. In its factual and theoretical
concerns, anthropology is a cumulative discipline in which
new discoveries give rise to new theories and these in turn
engender novel research projects. Yet, the actual field

experience is for each new recruit a unique and often regressive personal drama. This can be prepared for, but its full impact can never be precisely estimated in advance, nor can one say with complete confidence what the outcome will be.

These considerations, and the clearly critical significance of what we now know as "culture shock," naturally invite comparison to similar experiences in psychiatry and psycho-analysis.[10] There is certainly a valid sense in which "the field" is our equivalent of the analyst's couch, and the analogy between fieldwork and a training-analysis is obvious. It is also not difficult to see that the process of participant observation implies at least partial assimilation and internalization of the morality and assumptions of the alien society under study. S. T. Kimball, for instance, records how he encountered a ghost in the course of his fieldwork in Ireland, and how this helped to convince his hosts that he was a normal human being. I remember, too, how impressed I was when Paul Baxter told me how he had become so thoroughly imbued with the spirit of the Boran pastoralists he was studying in northern Kenya that he began to have Boran dreams. Similarly, Rosemary Firth reports how on the eve of her departure from Malaya, where she had been working with her husband, Raymond, she had a terrifying nightmare. She dreamed that she had become "a Malay peasant, a woman crouching over the fire to blow up the embers for an evening meal." She awoke, she records, "in terror, momentarily confused about her own identity – Malay woman or English scientist."[11]

Much of the terminology employed in the more reflective writing about fieldwork carries the same allusions. Evans-Pritchard (my teacher at Oxford) tells us that only the anthropologist, and not his hosts, can make the "transference" that is essential if fieldwork is to be successful.[12] The burden of anthropological discussion on this point, however, seems rather to follow Lévi-Strauss[13] in regarding the anthropologist as the equivalent of the analyst or psychiatrist, and the people studied as patients. Thus the onus of transference is shifted from the anthropologist to the people under study. But we need not be too perturbed by these strange transformations, for even psychoanalysts now officially recognize what they engagingly call "countertransference." This is the well-known process by which the analyst develops feelings towards the patients that are as ambivalent as their own toward the analyst. We also know, of course, that the boundary between patient and practitioner is, in the psychiatric field especially, not always clearly defined, and indeed is readily crossed in either direction.

These facts are more explicitly recognized in that older deviant cult that anthropologists call spirit-possession or shamanism, which I find a more illuminating model for both the psychoanalytic and the anthropological professions. Consider the parallels.[14] Like shamans, anthropologists go on trips to distant and mysterious worlds from which they bring back rich stores of exotic wisdom. They mediate between their own group and the unknown. They speak "with tongues" that are often unintelligible at home, and they act as mediums for the alien cultures through which they roam and which, in a sense, they come to incarnate. Like so many shamans or psychiatrists, they regularly occupy marginal positions in their own cultures as well as those they visit in search of knowledge.

Again, as was Malinowski, anthropologists are typically summoned suddenly and dramatically from other occupations and impelled to assume their true and final calling. Malinowski's whole system of graduate anthropological training was based on the shamanistic assumption that all his students were converts, inspired by Providence to enter into their true destiny. And this method was transferred lock, stock, and barrel to Oxford, where it was administered first by Radcliffe-Brown and then by Evans-Pritchard. This shamanistic tradition survives in the influentially held view (which I do not entirely share) that social anthropology should only be taught at the graduate level to mature students who have already been trained in another discipline.

Pursuing my parallel, we should note that in internalizing the culture of the alien hosts (as their client) the anthro-pologist becomes possessed by them. True, in common with shamans the world over, the anthropologist may dissemble and claim that he "possesses them," speaking suspiciously often of "*his* people." But do not be deceived. The real situation is that they possess him. Or rather, as in other possession cults, the situation is in reality ambiguous, each participant possessing the other (as in sexual intercourse). Finally, as the anthropologist proceeds to analyze and write up his findings, he externalizes his experience and gradually disengages himself from his informants. He reestablishes the original distance separating the two cultures. This process is a form of exorcism. And, as one would expect, as in shamanistic cults, the anthropologist rarely achieves a final and complete separation from his Muse. He instead remains in a permanent state of bondage, periodically seized and impelled to further bouts of exorcistic writing. Some, alas, are denied even this relief and remain so completely enthralled that they defy all attempts at exorcism, subsisting in what is virtually a perpetual state of mute communication with their muse.

III

It is now time to begin our careful scrutiny of the treasures that the anthropologist brings back from his shamanistic voyages. First, what psychiatrists would doubtless identify as our "primary" gains. If he had not acquired new information about a hitherto unrecorded or underrecorded culture, the anthropologist would have little to say. For, of course, we are all plagiarists, *bricoleurs*, living parasitically upon our ethnographic sources. Where would Malinowski have got without the Trobriand Islanders, Evans-Pritchard without the Nuer and Zande, Firth without the Tikopia, or Forde without the Yako? All our pronouncements carry conviction and authenticity only when we anchor them in the lives and thoughts of those we study. Our ethnographic sources provide our indispensable claims to legitimacy; they establish our credentials: "The Nuer do that, you say"; "How odd, the Somali don't"; and so on.

This ultimate referring of all our ideas to the ethnographic "facts" elucidated by painstaking field research is now so deeply engrained in our subject and so taken for granted that we tend to forget how dependent we are on our sources. Acutely aware of the subjectivity of our research techniques, we tend now to overestimate our part and to underestimate that of our informants. Strange as it may seem, the same tendency toward a position of ethnocentric superiority seems to me implicit in the rather overworked view of anthropology as the spoiled child of Western imperialism. Here those anthropologists who carried out research in the colonial territories are depicted as the deliberate – or, more charitably, unwitting – instruments of imperialism. These circumstances, it is held, have led those who undertook their fieldwork during that period to misunderstand the real position of their subjects and thus to have produced inevitably distorted analyses of social structures and cultures.

I find the condescending implications of this interpretation repugnant. It assumes that the people we study, or have studied, possess no vigor of their own; that they have insipid lackluster cultures with no intrinsic dynamism, no élan vital, no capacity for self-expression; and that such articulate representatives as anthropologists encounter are by definition not representative but, on the contrary, brainwashed slaves and Uncle Toms. Those who paint this misleading picture, it must be acknowledged, have usually not carried out actual fieldwork and tend to overgeneralize from the deplorable treatment of the American Indians in North and South America.[15] But they are also, I think, victims of a wider ethnocentric tendency to exaggerate greatly the force and finality of European culture and its implicit as well as explicit assumptions. Whatever Durkheim may have said, the people we study are *not* robots. Unlike artists' models, they do not posture pliantly as the omniscient ethnographer wields his brilliant brush. Cultures do *not* pose as "models" for the anthropologist in the servile, manipulable fashion that artists typically expect of their subjects. Excessive preoccupation with so-called theoretical models conceals, very conveniently, our own lack of originality and the contrasting richness of the peoples we study. It is *we*, not *they*, who are the puppets. Let me offer some evidence to support this heterodox view.

First let us take the instructive case of Lévi-Strauss. There exists a large and often tedious exegetical (I almost said liturgical) literature on this brilliant man's thoughts and their intellectual pedigree (much of which he himself has disowned).[16] But whatever the obvious influences of Hegel, Marx, and Freud on the development of Lévi-Strauss's ideas, there is also a quite remarkable concordance between his key concepts and the salient characteristics of the ethnographic area in which he has actually carried out field research. As is well known, the colonial history of the American Indians is a sorry tale of rapacious exploitation and extermination. Those Indians who were not killed outright by the conquerors had their numbers dramatically reduced by exotic new diseases and related calamities. The surviving remnants of indigenous culture were then further impoverished and diluted by foreign accretions, with which in some cases they combined to produce bizarre hybrids. The presence today of Indian themes in the increasingly popular syncretic cults of the American continent bears impressive witness both to the vitality and persistence of Indian culture and to the centuries of intense pressure its authentic bearers have been forced to endure. Counterculture is a much older phenomenon in America than is generally supposed.

From the anthropological point of view, the colonization of America thus produced a bewildering assortment of ethnographic jigsaw puzzles. This encouraged those who sought to solve them to concentrate on what Robert Murphy has called the "cultural residues of the mind," as they attempted to wring out the last pieces of remembered custom from the oldest Indian informants they could find. As Murphy observes, it also prompted the publication of a series of monographs that, in their exhaustive cataloguing of disparate and often disjointed cultural elements, read like laundry lists.[17] These circumstances strikingly reflect Robert Lowie's famous definition of civilization as a "thing of shreds and patches."[18] They also, I suggest, directly reflect Lévi-Strauss's conception of primitives as *bricoleurs*, wayward beachcombers picking up and ingeniously recombining the strangely assorted treasures deposited on the sands by the successive tides of different cultures and civilizations. The same formative forces seem equally influential in the development of Lévi-Strauss's concepts of structure and structuralism and in his confusing contrast between what he calls "mechanical" and "statistical" models. An area so littered with various marinaded culture elements, and belonging as much to archaeology as to ethnography, prompted an earlier generation of anthropologists to explain the similarities between one culture-complex and another in terms of diffusion from a common original source. It is a very small step indeed from this to the cerebral geology of Lévi-Strauss and his quest for "unconscious structures," and one that fits the conditions of the area just as closely as the earlier diffusionist approach. Indeed, this transformation from diffusionism to structuralism is virtually explicit in some of the great master's writing.[19]

Let me turn now to examples of the same ethnographic imperialism from the British tradition of structural-functionalism. In recent years it has become increasingly evident that the theoretical interests of Africanist anthropologists – particularly their emphasis on corporate kinship groups, segmentary lineage systems, and centralized kingdoms – reflect local African cultural particularities. Generalizing theoretical models based on this work do not always travel as well as many had hoped. As Anthony Forge demonstrated so effectively in his 1971 Malinowski Lecture, New Guinea is in many respects a test case for anthropological theory. Difficulties over the importation there of Africanist models that have clearly suffered on the long sea-crossing sharpen our growing awareness of the extent to which much of our theorizing is influenced by the areas in which we carry out research.[20] Ah, those treacherous coral reefs! Similar compatibility problems arise when other ethnographic regions join the debate. It is now pretty clear, for instance, that the long controversy between Meyer Fortes and Edmund Leach at Cambridge over the relative significance of ties based on

descent and those created by marriage is in large measure an
issue between the Tallensi of northern Ghana and the Kachins
of Burma. The former project an image of the ineluctable
nature of kinship in blood. The latter are essentially alliance
theorists who suppose that because in their case it is more
honorable, and therefore more prestigious, to give than to
receive wives, so it must be for all mankind. (The Kachins are,
of course, mistaken on this point, as a number of Leach's
colleagues have not hesitated to point out.)

But perhaps the most striking examples of this process in
the *belle époque* of British social anthropology derive from the
work of Evans-Pritchard and reflect his charisma as a teacher.
Thus the lineages he discovered in the minds of the Nuer of
the Sudan have been transported around the globe by his
disciples and students. In the same way, the contrast he found
in Zande conceptions between witchcraft as a psychic force
and sorcery as a magical technique has assumed the status of
a universally valid categorical distinction, one that has been
applied indiscriminately elsewhere. It is also one of the
cornerstones of several fashionable anthropological theories
of religion and cosmology. The plain fact is, however, that
most religions that include analogous beliefs in mystical
malevolence do not make the Zande distinction, which is
actually the exception rather than the rule. Are there no
limits, one might ask, to Zande cultural imperialism?

It will be evident, I hope, that although diffusionism may
have withered away as an acceptable theoretical pursuit, like
other banished ghosts it still haunts the minds of anthropologists. It is, in fact, the main mechanism by which the
cultures we study in one place influence what our students
search for in another. To an important extent, anthropology is
indeed the "translation of culture," in the sense that the
anthropologist picks up ideas in one place and unloads them
in another. For this reason, following his own experience of
two contrasting African cultures, Evans-Pritchard used to
exhort his students to study more than one society. But even
this may not suffice. So, with commendable candor, Max
Gluckman confesses that his stimulating comparative analysis

of rebellion in tribal states has been weakened by what he terms "the ethnocentrism bred by studying Zulu and Barotse."[21]

IV

Anthropological analyses, for all our fine talk, thus inevitably bear the stamp of the cultures in which they have been forged. But there is more to the plagiarism than this. It is not only what both the Dogon and Professor Lévi-Strauss would call "surface structures" that are thus appropriated and thrust into general theoretical currency. We must also consider the role of what are sometimes known technically (and revealingly) as "key informants." Our dependence, at least in the elucidation of certain topics, on such figures is sometimes explicitly acknowledged. So, for instance, Stanner describes the special relationship he developed with an Australian aborigine informant who was unusually gifted in employing homemade visual models to illustrate the structure of his society. Stanner reports how he eventually turned one of the old aborigine's demonstrations (in which sticks were used as counters and stick movements as signs of marriage, parentage, residence, and descent) into models for teaching the theory of the aboriginal subsection system "much as they teach it."[22] With equal frankness, Raymond Firth records his debt to a particular Tikopia friend with whom he enjoyed a unique relationship and who contributed more than any other informant to his understanding of Tikopia society and culture. Anthony Forge pays similar tribute to the would-be Big-Man he encountered as a fellow stranger in the village that was his base in New Guinea, acknowledging the theoretical insight he gained from their discussions about the nature of power and authority among the Abelam.

Discounting Carlos Castaneda, the most outstanding examples on record of such fecund friendships with informants are almost certainly those of Victor Turner and Marcel Griaule; and they concern, as might be expected, the interpretation of religion and ritual. Turner's impressively documented analysis of the symbolism of the Ndembu people of central Africa is firmly anchored in a virtually unique apparatus of indigenous exegesis. This work is clearly based on months of painstaking observation and on commentaries from a multitude of independent sources obtained, wherever possible, in ritual contexts. Nevertheless, Turner has not hesitated to acknowledge his special debt to the magician Muchona (nicknamed "The Hornet"), who more than any other person guided him through the Ndembu forest of symbols. This imaginative interpreter of Ndembu symbolism and a friendly Ndembu mission teacher formed with Turner an impromptu field seminar or workshop, which, over a period of many months, pondered the inner mysteries of Ndembu religion and ritual. As Turner puts it, Muchona "delighted in making explicit what he had known subliminally about his own religion." Like his European colleague, but for different reasons, Muchona – who was frail, somewhat effeminate, and of slave origin – was in many respects an outsider, a marginal man capable of considering objectively what most Ndembu simply took for granted.[23]

Griaule's case is the more remarkable if for no other reason than that his dialogue with the blind Dogon sage Ogotommeli lasted thirty-three successive days and led to the production of that unique anthropological document, *Dieu d'Eau* (English version: *Conversations with Ogotommeli*). After fifteen years of intermittent research among this famous west African people of the Niger, it was Griaule's chance encounter with Ogotommeli that led him to the final breakthrough into the inner mysteries of Dogon cosmology. In their sustained and highly sophisticated discussions, all the barriers separating the great French ethnographer and his brilliant *equipe* of younger workers from their final conquest of the deep structures of Dogon thought and myth were at last overcome. Ogotommeli himself died in 1947. He did not live to see the book Griaule had written about him or the further progress of the French team's research. "His death," as Griaule sadly remarked at the time, was a "serious loss to humane studies." This tribute he was quick to qualify by adding, "not that the blind old man was the only one to know the doctrine of his people."[24]

Such examples illustrate the extent to which fieldwork is essentially a creative exchange. They also emphasize that it is a very unlucky field-worker who does not discover at least one local counterpart to help him with his task. These situations are, I believe, much more common than one might gather from much anthropological writing. Moreover, when they are acknowledged, the tendency is to present such encounters as exchanges in which the anthropologist inevitably plays the dominant role, so that the outcome cannot but be a tribute to his ingenuity and originality rather than to that of his informants. So, for instance, the suspicion lingers in many quarters that, having posed the appropriate philosophical questions, Griaule induced Ogotommeli to improvise an ad hoc philosophy, substantially a synthesis of elements from both their cultures rather than an authentic Dogon product. English commentators, at any rate, seem generally to see the result as a collaborative work of art in which it is difficult to disentangle the respective contributions of the two artists. This view recalls that enshrined in one splendidly egotistical passage in the first volume of *Mythologiques*, where Lévi-Strauss declares, "It is immaterial whether . . . the thought processes of the South American Indians take shape through the medium of my thought, or whether mine take place through the medium of theirs."[25]

v

Whatever the real balance of invention and creativity in these and comparable instances, we now turn to less obvious forms of anthropological plagiarism – cases in which, sometimes unwittingly, the ethnographer lifts from anonymous informants not only his many-layered factual data but also his *theoretical* interpretations. I begin with a case in which the interpretation is virtually explicit in the ethnographic "facts" themselves. It is much to her credit that Mary Douglas makes no attempt to disguise the ultimate ethnographic source of her contributions to anthropological theory. In the heady atmosphere of contemporary theorizing on the nature of cosmologies, however, it is often difficult to remember that the genesis of Douglas's stimulating ideas on dangerous anomalies reaches back, beyond William James and Leviticus, to the humble Lele of the Kasai in the Congo and to their taxonomic treatment of that fascinating creature, the scaly anteater (or, to be more accurate, of one of the two local varieties).[26] As Douglas records, the Lele describe the pangolin in such a way that there can be no "mistaking its anomalous character." The Lele say, "In our forest there is an animal with the body and tail of a fish, covered with scales. It has four legs, and it climbs on trees." It is also symbolically connected with fertility, being the object of a fertility cult, and in this context the Lele observe that like humans (but unlike other animals) the pangolin parsimoniously produces only one offspring at a time. So, as Mary Douglas points out, it is not difficult to see that pangolins are comparable to humans in the way that the overfecund parents of twins resemble animals. From this point of departure, Professor Douglas's fertile imagination moves quickly to the biblical abominations, on which she is able to shed new light, and thence to the more general explanatory concept of "matter out of place" (recalling Shaw's famous definition of obscenity), and finally to an elaborate general theory of mystical danger in which Lele ethnography is left far behind – for their ethnographer has, as it were, moved on and up into different intellectual circles. Those who disagree with her views may feel that the Lele have much to answer for!

Now to return to the work of Victor Turner among the Ndembu. Ndembu men pay their women the doubtful compliment of tracing all their important kinship links matrilineally. But in return they expect wives to leave their maternal kin and homes to live in the settlements of their husbands. This practice separates mature women from their nearest kin and especially from their brothers, for whom they provide heirs. These mundane events do not go unnoticed by the spirits. Women are regularly plagued by disease-bearing spirits that "catch" them causing much inconvenience and suffering. Ndembu explain that the spirits strike their human prey because they are angry at being "forgotten," and in these circumstances it scarcely comes as a surprise to learn that the spirits involved are usually from the mother's side of the family. So, as Turner analytically expresses it, apparently paraphrasing the Ndembu, these women's spirit afflictions serve as a sharp and salutary reminder "that their own first loyalty is to their maternal villages and that they bear children not for their husbands but for their brothers back home."[27]

This example prompts consideration of a wider series of issues connected with the anthropologist's treatment of other people's mystical beliefs. As is well known, spirits and dreams are often loosely associated; indeed, one of the main Victorian intellectualist explanations for the existence of beliefs in spirits and spiritual activity traced their origin to dreams. The intellectual patent for this interpretation is usually, although not universally or unequivocally, assigned by anthropologists to Frazer's contemporary Sir Edward Tylor. Tylor's views on the subject, which have been widely condemned as absurdly simplistic, have passed into the anthropological literature only to pass out of it, with a few accompanying valedictory messages. Speaking for many of his colleagues, Evans-Pritchard castigates Tylor's theory as an explanation of the "if I were a horse" variety, the implication being that it was Tylor, not the savage, who made spirits out of dreams.[28] Even without psychoanalytic theory or the evidence of psychiatrists, however, there is actually a great mass of ethnographic data showing clearly and unambiguously that – with all due respect to Evans-Pritchard – Tylor's interpretation is, up to a point, good horse sense. Like so many of our own lay countrymen, the peoples we study do attach a great deal of importance to their dreams and explicitly adduce dream experience as evidence for the existence of the spirits in which they believe. This is ethnographic fact, not Tylorean fantasy.

Moreover, highly sophisticated subtleties are employed to create and sustain the links between dreams and spirits. Raymond Firth, for instance, speaking from a rationalist point of view, reports that the "Tikopia belief that the figure seen in a dream is not a human being but an impersonation of him by a spirit" disposes of naïve attempts to disprove the actuality of dreams by confronting the person dreamed of with the contents of the dream.[29] (Godfrey Lienhardt's detailed account of the complex metaphysical significance of dreams for the Dinka is also apposite here.)[30] The quotation from Firth recalls the intriguing discussion between the Dogon philosopher Ogotommeli and the French ethnographer Griaule on the subject of the narrow steps of the Dogon heavenly house – how could they possibly accommodate the vast numbers of animals their cosmology required them to support? With its echoes of angels dancing on pinheads, the question has a familiar ring; and so has Ogotommeli's answer. As he explained, the animals involved were all symbols, and "any number of symbols could find room on a one-cubit step"![31]

Let us now turn to another area where there is an intriguing interplay between mystical beliefs and anthropological theory. It is generally recognized that one of the most impressive accomplishments of anthropological analysis is its elucidation of the "problem of witchcraft" – a subject Maurice Freedman has aptly described as an "anthropologist's paradise." As we now understand, witchcraft provides an indispensable component in many philosophies of misfortune. It is the friend rather than the foe of morality, which it supports and even sometimes sanctions by attacking only those whose moral imperfections expose them to its effects. And, in its actualization in witchcraft accusations, it offers a convenient means of ventilating those pressures and tensions that are, as it were, part of the opportunity cost of close-knit communal life everywhere. From this perspective witchcraft is manifestly the pseudonym for jealousy and envy, and the means by which these antisocial sentiments are made to bear the burden of life's inequalities. These insights have enabled anthropologists to achieve a deeper understanding of the composite structure and complex workings of religion and ideology generally. They also, of course, have corroborated much of the psychodynamic approach to interpersonal tensions in psychiatry – where the terminology is a bit different, but the sentiments much the same.

This has not passed unnoticed. There is, nevertheless, a certain irony in the position concerning this parallelism taken by some psychiatrists. Professor Ari Kiev, a leading American authority on the subject, solemnly warns that, in view of the similarity between the two theories, caution should be exercised in introducing the psychodynamic approach in certain cultures lest traditional witchcraft beliefs be reinforced.[32] Some members of other disciplines are more accepting. A number of historians, and none more impressively than Keith Thomas and Alan MacFarlane, have taken these simple anthropological discoveries to heart and applied them effectively to many traditionally neglected and undervalued aspects of the beliefs of our own ancestors.[33] Those embarrassingly irrational superstitions of earlier generations gain a new lease of life when set in the wider context of meaning disclosed by anthropology.

My interest here, however, is simply in tracing the intellectual pedigree of these influential theories that attempt to explain witchcraft. The orthodox genealogy takes us back to Evans-Pritchard's analysis of Zande witchcraft[34] and to his remarkable mind – or perhaps more daringly to meetings between his mind and those of the Zande he knew well. But this is only half the story. We can go much farther and say that certain Zande – princes standing outside the vicious circle of witchcraft accusations, for instance, and other similarly detached informants – were as acutely aware as Evans-Pritchard of the scapegoating functions of witchcraft accusations and of the explanatory convenience of the beliefs themselves. Evans-Pritchard does not disguise this. Indeed, one of the most striking merits of his study lies precisely in his detailed examination and exposition of the points of convergence and divergence between his analysis of Zande beliefs and that made in different circumstances by various categories of Zande themselves. Other peoples with similar confidence in the efficacy of mystical malevolence have shown that they do not lag far behind the Zande or their ethnographer in appreciating what *really* underlies their beliefs.

I am not, of course, claiming that these indigenous analyses of the operation and significance of such major cultural phenomena as witchcraft beliefs necessarily coincide exactly with the "objective" picture that the anthropologist can elicit from a meticulous investigation of actual case histories. But I do hold that, at the very least, they constitute a kind of metatheory providing many essential clues, and that they are consequently the original, if modest, sources of much that passes for advanced anthropological theory.

Nor is it only in the field of witchcraft that our subjects are so gifted in self-analysis and so generous with their theoretical insights! Much the same often applies to the study of other religious phenomena. I once had the good fortune, for example, to meet a Somali tribesman who gave me an impeccably Durkheimian explanation of the function of the traditional ancestor cult in terms of the social euphoria generated by commemorative feasts at the ancestors' shrines (see Chapter 8). Again, it is not without significance that my interpretation of spirit-possession cults in terms of women's liberation (Chapter 3) partly derived from the manipulated men who have to bear most of the heavy costs and other inconveniences involved. Men's awareness of what their spirit-ridden wives are up to is, as will be shown, not limited to the Somali among whom I worked but seems to occur in most of the other officially male-dominated cultures where the same cults flourish.[35]

VI

These deeper instances of anthropological indebtedness raise two connected theoretical issues. The first and less significant, except methodologically, is the key importance of the skeptical informant who, being partly external to, or unconcerned in, a given situation, can stand back from it and take a more dispassionate, and in our terms "objective," view of what is happening. Skepticism clearly is not necessarily a full-time intellectual or emotional occupation. It is often simply a function of an individual's lack of direct involvement in particular circumstances. The wider and more interesting problem is that of determining, defining, and adequately describing what exactly it is that people do believe. If beliefs that ostensibly say one thing are widely understood to mean another, how do we assess them? How are we to price beliefs that regularly circulate at well below their face value? What is the relationship between the official and unofficial currencies, between the standard exchange rate and that on the black market? Where or when does belief become half-belief, and half-belief in turn become make-belief or dis-belief? Evans-Pritchard's exposition of Zande beliefs in witchcraft and magic will serve to clarify my difficulty. In a discussion that seems unconsciously to commemorate Freud, Evans-Pritchard shows clearly how Zande dispose of the problem created for them when their mystical techniques fail. Take a typical example: A witch doctor's diagnosis is falsified by subsequent developments. Zande conclude, very reasonably, that the doctor is a quack and should have his name struck off the register of authorized practitioners. He is no good because, obviously, he lacks sufficient knowledge of the mystical techniques necessary for effective work in his specialty. It is man, not magic, that is imperfect; and such particularistic confrontations between objective reality and the eternal Zande verities are, therefore, not of the kind to inaugurate scientific revolutions. Individual shortcomings do not threaten general truths, which bounce back, as it were, with renewed vigor. Evans-Pritchard sums up this familiar situation in a succinct formula: faith tempered by skepticism.

But this is not the problem to which I wish to call attention. My difficulty is the reverse of this: Why do people go on believing in *individual instances* of (let us say) witchcraft when in general they know that witchcraft is not quite what it seems? If everybody is consciously aware that witchcraft is really a flag of convenience for the powerful tides of jealousy and aggression that well up from the unconscious, why not fly the true colors? Many anthropologists offer an answer, one that I consider partial, misleading, and contrary to the ethnographic facts.[36] This explanation maintains that witchcraft acts as a surrogate for envy and spite in contexts where the open acknowledgment of these emotions cannot possibly be contemplated. So, it is held, witchcraft conceals and mystifies hatred. But how can it possibly do this, if everyone knows that it is hatred? Are the Zande and other peoples with comparable beliefs so benighted that they are exempt from even the most elementary Freudian principles about the relationship between conscious and unconscious affect? Of course not; but perhaps we can now identify our situation more precisely. Surely it is analogous to that frequently encountered in modern psychiatry, where, with the wide diffusion of Freud's teaching and of popular psychodynamic concepts among the laity, many patients not only possess insight into their own problems but are as fully versed in the technical jargon as their therapists. Or, to put it in a more ancient formulation: The Devil knows well how to quote Scripture for his own purposes. Such cases are, of course, notoriously difficult to treat. Can we then say that here again faith is tempered by skepticism? Or would it be better to say that skepticism is tempered by faith? When, to return to our original question, does skepticism overwhelm faith completely? What do people *really* believe and feel?

This remains our oldest and most refractory problem. The classical example in the empiricist fieldwork tradition is Malinowski's "discovery" that his Trobriand Islanders seemed to live in sexual innocence, touchingly believing that their wives were impregnated by spirits. This, at any rate, was the official doctrine in this matrilineal society. But did the Trobriand Islanders really believe it, or was it mere dogma to which reluctant and skeptical lip service was paid in appropriate circumstances? The difficulty of answering questions of this kind, posed in this way, is clearly shown in the wide-ranging controversy provoked by Edmund Leach's stimulating resurrection of this whole issue in his Henry Myers Lecture on "Virgin Birth."[37] Further evidence can be found in the parallel argument between Evans-Pritchard and Raymond Firth[38] on the interpretation of the relationship between twins and birds postulated by the Nuer, Tikopia, and other peoples. These fairly specific examples, moreover, are part of the wider and continuing debate regarding the structure of traditional or "primitive" thought and the many attempts to specify, analyze, and compare cosmologies. The immense popularity that Lévi-Strauss's opaque disquisitions on mythology enjoy is itself an excellent measure of the topicality of the problem.

VII

Despite so much devoted and learned attention, however, the answer to our question "What do people really believe . . . " is still decidedly problematical.[39] In my opinion, we have scarcely advanced beyond the achievements of Evans-Pritchard's study of Zande witchcraft. And if we still have difficulty in satisfactorily exposing the beliefs of a given people, how can we possibly embark on comparative studies of different cosmologies? Progress here is often impeded by our failure to appreciate clearly what we are trying to do. We constantly seek to leap precipitately from the concrete and particular to the abstract and general. We aspire to identify and characterize a whole people's philosophy or "world view" and to say – as we so glibly do – that one culture is more or less pious (or mystical, or ritualistic, etc.) than another. Such cardboard cosmological portraits are often just as treacherous and misleading as those that seek to depict national character (see Chapter 6). We also regularly forget what, as I have tried to show, we are forced to acknowledge when we frankly consider the true sources of our information: that faith and skepticism and various degrees of reliance on mystical or nonmystical comforts are functions of situations and circumstances. A complete inventory of the explanatory beliefs (mystical and nonmystical) available in a given culture is thus meaningless unless accompanied by a minutely detailed exposition of their deployment in actual situations, sufficiently well specified to permit rigorous comparison in other cultures. The detachment of beliefs from their ambient circumstances produces gross distortion and misunderstanding. "There are no atheists in the trenches." Again, as everybody knows, but we as anthropologists too readily forget, the passage of time is another critical variable affecting explanations of the same event (as it is reevaluated) by the same actors in the same culture at different stages in the unfolding social drama that accompanies it. Thus characterizations of the patterns of causal explanations offered for an illness or misfortune must specify the time span within which they are effective. Obviously, the same symptoms may be explained in different ways according to their temporal persistence. What accounts satisfactorily for the transient appearance of a malady is unlikely to serve to explain its persistence in a chronic form, and so on.

Those who perceive the full magnitude of the task involved here tend, understandably enough, to shrink from it, and even to give up all hope of ever achieving valid comparisons in this field of study. Other, sturdier scholars, undaunted by these dangers, bravely struggle on, sometimes – as in the case of Mary Douglas[40] – at the price of trailing off into clouds of incomprehensible whimsy. It is abundantly clear that we urgently need a more discriminating and rigorous analytical apparatus to collect and codify case histories exhibiting the actual, selective use of explanatory principles over time in clearly specified and accurately observed conditions. This is asking much. But I believe it is not impossible, and I cite as an example Gilbert Lewis's pioneering ethnomedical study of the Gnau people of the western Sepik region of New Guinea.[41] In this detailed and fully circumstantial account of the recognition of, and response to, sickness, we find precisely the kind and range of information that is essential if we are to achieve valid comparative studies of what people really think and feel. If other anthropologists were to follow this exacting example we would soon have a useful body of evidence; we could control the relevant variables and successfully compare like with like to discover the real cultural variations in response to affliction. From this starting point we could move on to a wider, objectively based comparative cosmology resting not on impressionistic summaries or "condensations" but on rigorously controlled point-by-point comparisons. I do not claim that the arguments deployed in subsequent chapters always meet these requirements, but I hope that they at least point in this direction.

CHAPTER 2

The spirit spider
and the pangolin

I

In her seminal essay on Lele religious symbolism, Mary Douglas (1957) rightly observed that, in order to be effective, symbols do not need to be grounded in objectively accurate knowledge and may indeed be based on mistaken information. So, in the case of animals selected to act as symbols, what matters is not actual animal behavior but rather the characteristics and properties imputed to them by those who employ them as symbols. The famous *tarantismo* spider cult of southern Italy shows how this dictum may sometimes be applicable at one level while not applying at others. The tarantula spirit spider in Apulia (the region containing the eponymous town of Taranto) has potentially two types of actual tarantula spider (*Latrodectus* and *Lycosa*) with which it might be identified, but only one (*Lycosa*) is selected as the actual counterpart for the spirit. The spider (*Latrodectus*) which is passed over is, paradoxically, armed with a toxic bite capable of indeed causing the symptoms associated with tarantism. This situation of two similar zoological categories, only one of which receives ritual attention, has parallels in Lele animal symbolism (and is not unknown elsewhere). Douglas bases her famous analysis of the "anomalous" pangolin on one type (*Manis tricuspis*) and rather passes over the other pangolin (*Manis gigantea*) which is also found among the Lele. As we shall see, this raises questions about the adequacy of her anomaly argument and invites further consideration of her data. More generally, where such pairs of related zoological avatars are subject to such

26

differential symbolization this offers a unique opportunity to test the validity of theories of symbolization. A fully satisfactory interpretation should be able to explain the circumstances in which one of the pair is chosen at the expense of the other.

With its roots in the middle ages, tarantism survives on a reduced scale in parts of contemporary southern Italy where the classical study of the phenomenon was made by the pioneer of Italian ethno-sociology (the precursor of social anthropology in Italy), Ernesto de Martino (1961) and his team. Here the cult typically involves women who are recruited by being bitten by the tarantula "spider" and seek a cure in domestic rituals, conducted with the appropriate musical accompaniment (tarantella); or at Christian shrines such as that in St Paul's chapel at Galatina in Salente (Apulia), which was studied by de Martino and his colleagues (for more recent research, see Montinaro 1976; Castiglione 1977). The symptoms of the affliction which, in its acute phase, may include dizziness, weakness, feelings of anguish, psychomotor agitation, stomach and muscular pains, nausea and increased erotic appetite, are attributed to the bite of the tarantula. In Apulia there are two main types of actual tarantula: *Lycosa* and *Latrodectus*, the first of which, although armed with a savage bite, is essentially harmless. *Latrodectus*, in contrast, while not particularly aggressive and usually only attacking people when they inadvertently brush against it, is small and slow-moving but much more dangerous. Disarmingly, its bite is not immediately very painful at the location of the bite and may thus pass unnoticed for some time. However, although rarely fatal, the toxins injected by the bite have a powerful psychotropic effect, producing the symptoms mentioned above and causing the victim to feel severely ill for several days (de Martino 1961: 78; cf. Gallini 1967: 278ff.).

II

Although the behavior and symptoms *actually* produced by *Latrodectus* are thus closely similar to those in the acute phases of tarantism, this spider is *not* directly implicated in the cult. Members of the cult, initiated by a "spider's bite," have not actually been bitten by this dangerous spider. As de Martino has elegantly demonstrated, the "bite" which they have experienced is a symbolic or mythical construct which can recur at different stages in the life of the afflicted victim and may even run in families. It usually first occurs, and may recur, when the victim is subject to exceptional stress and personal difficulty. Initiation into this "cult of affliction" (cf. Lewis 1989: 59ff.) thus assumes the form of symptoms of illness and distress which are interpreted as signs of the tarantula spirit's attack. Although through their agricultural work in the fields, men are in fact more prone to be bitten by the toxic *Latrodectus* spider, it is paradoxically the less directly exposed women who are the chief victims of tarantism in Apulia. Those so afflicted formerly sought relief in healing rituals, danced to the tune of the tarantella in the patient's own home. Today, however, recourse is more usually had in Apulia to the chapel of St Paul at the church in Galatina where exorcistic rituals are celebrated each year on the feast days of St Paul (28 and 29 June). Here, in June 1959 when they visited it, de Martino and his team found that thirty-two out of thirty-seven victims seeking relief from the spider's bite were women. Following the legend of St Paul's eradication of venomous creatures in Malta, the unique curative role of this shrine is based on the myth of the Apostle's travels in Italy and the hospitable reception he received at Galatina – in return for which he obtained blessings from God to cure those bitten by snakes, scorpions, and tarantulas.

This symbolic bite is administered by a symbolic tarantula which in local belief in Apulia assumes various sizes and colors and dances to different tarantula tunes. The spider's "bite" is closely related to its size and energy and it passes on its specific characteristics to its victim. Each with its own personal name (e.g., Rosina, Peppina, Maria Antonietta), there are thus dancing and singing tarantulas; some excite their victims to melancholy, others to joy, aggression, or erotic behavior. Whatever its specific features, the tarantula introduces into the veins of its human prey a "poison" which is believed to persist as long as the spider lives (and this symbolic tarantula is considerably longer-lived than its zoological equivalent). To achieve a measure of relief, the possessed victim (for that is her condition) must perform the "dance of the little spider" (the tarantella), dancing "as the victim possessed by the beast and as a heroine who forces it to dance with her" (de Martino 1961: 63). The possessed person argues with the spider, sometimes submitting to its demands and sometimes forcing it to submit until finally agreement is reached between them on the duration of the ritual and the timing of the next crisis. Once relief has been obtained for the time being, the grateful victim pays homage to St Paul at his shrine in Galatia.

A typical case discussed by de Martino (1961: 73ff.) in some detail illustrates the process involved here. Maria, whose father had died when she was thirteen years old, was brought up by an aunt and uncle who lived in straitened circumstances. At the age of eighteen, Maria fell in love with a young man whose family disapproved of the relationship because of her poverty and who subsequently abandoned her.

She suffered much from this disappointment. One Sunday while gazing pensively out of her window, Maria was suddenly "bitten" by the spider and felt impelled to dance. About the same time, a woman who lived nearby began to regard Maria, despite her affliction, as a suitable bride for her son who was ill and often out of work. Mother and son accompanied Maria to the chapel at Galatina to pay homage to the saint and the mother took the opportunity of asking Maria if she would accept her son as husband. To gain time, still fascinated by her first love and not attracted by this proposal, Maria pleaded that she had not sufficient resources for a trousseau because of the cost of treatment for her tarantism.

At this point, St Paul providentially appeared, ordering Maria not to marry, and summoning her to join him in a mystical union. Shortly afterwards, however, the son and his mother succeeded in luring Maria out to a deserted farm and forced her to live there in shame. After a little time, a quarrel

occurred when her mortal spouse brusquely ordered her to
iron his clothes. As she went out to return the iron she had
borrowed from a neighbor, she met St Peter and St Paul who
said to her: "Leave the iron and come with us." When Maria
responded, "And my husband, what of him?," she was told not
to worry on that account. This incident occurred on a Sunday
at exactly the time of day at which she had first been "bitten"
by the spider. After encountering the saint, Maria disappeared
for three days, wandering in the fields. St Paul, annoyed that
she had disobeyed his order not to marry, allowed her to be
"bitten" this second time, forcing her to dance for nine days.
Reminded of her holy tryst by this strange love-bite, Maria
eventually achieved a compromise between the rival interests
of her human and spiritual spouses. She agreed to a formal
marriage with her human seducer while continuing to
celebrate her spiritual union by an annual recurrence of her
possession affliction in time to participate in the ceremonies
on the Saint's feast-day.

So, driven by circumstances to marry a man she did not
want, Maria continued to pay periodical tribute to the
tarantula and to the saint, reviving on each occasion, in
the symbolism of the rite, the original adventure of the bite of
love and being cured at the same time through the grace of her
celestial husband. What had begun as an affliction attributed
to the demonic spider, had found its apotheosis in a peculiarly
intimate communion with St Paul. While Maria was thus able
to control her illness through her annual participation in the
Pauline rites at Galatina, this whole pattern of behavior was
highly expressive of her plight. Through these recurrent
outbreaks, followed by treatment at the shrine, Maria was able
to sustain her condemnation of her forced marriage, making
conjugal life difficult, imposing severe economic stress on the
family which she did not love, and flagrantly calling public
attention to her problems. If she could not radically remedy
her situation, at least she could continue to protest at it in
a religious idiom which men could condone as divinely sanc-
tioned therapy (cf. de Martino, *passim*, and Lewis 1989: 80–3).

The figure of St Paul here is extremely ambivalent. As

might be anticipated, the Apostle is credited with causing the spirit-spider affliction he cures. On the one hand, there is the benevolent figure of St Paul, protector and healer of those bitten by the spider; on the other, there is a punitive St Paul who sends the tarantula to bite sinners. There is further the hybrid figure of St Paul-the-tarantula, or the tarantula-St Paul, which appears in the course of the exorcistic rites where the possessed victim speaks both as the tarantula and as St Paul. This identification is furthered in the experience of those women bitten by the spider who may have visions and dreams of St Paul, summoning them to mystical marriage. Earthier relations are suggested in the ribald invocations addressed by the afflicted women at his shrine: "My St Paul of the Tarantists who pricks the girls in their vaginas" (de Martino 1961: 122).

III

Having established the main features of the culturally constructed symbolic spider and its bite, we return to examine its relationship to the two real tarantula spiders which actually occur locally. As we have seen, although the highly toxic bite of *Latrodectus* can produce symptoms which are typical of the initial and acute phases of the symbolic "bite," this spider is paradoxically not directly implicated. On the contrary, the tarantula which is identified as the natural species whose bite is believed to cause spider possession is the *Lycosa* tarantula, a large black, hairy spider with menacing claws. This spider sleeps in an underground nest for most of the day, but at night it ranges widely in search of food. It weaves no web and moves rapidly, pursuing its victims vigorously and rearing up in an impressively aggressive manner as it closes in on its prey. The immediate local effects of its bite are more painful than those of *Latrodectus* which is a less visually striking and smaller spider, moving more sluggishly and less aggressively, and waiting for its prey at the centre of its web. Both spiders are quiescent during the winter and active in the summer when they mate and reproduce.

Although it might be claimed that *Lycosa* receives attention because it does not spin a web and so is an "anomalous" spider, there is no indication that this is regarded as a notable feature. Rather, it seems clear that the features which actually attract attention are not this but its size, aggression, and sharp bite and that, on these grounds, it acquires symbolic salience as the zoological counterpart of the spirit spider. That the absence of a web is not of mystical import is also suggested by the fact that the spirit spider in the local tarantist ideology *is* endowed with a strong web which traps its victims, leaving them suspended to swing helplessly in the air with the wind (de Martino 1961: 61). De Martino thus seems perfectly correct to argue that the spirit spider is in fact a composite construction, drawing on the zoological characteristics and behavior of both *Lycosa* and *Latrodectus*, though "preferentially orientated" toward the former with its instantly impressive bite. The psychic crisis itself, however, nevertheless follows the pattern of the symptomology of the toxic bite of *Latrodectus*. The potentially generative effect of the *Latrodectus* bite seems confirmed by a case involving a *male* victim which de Martino (1961: 81) reports. Here a man was bitten by *Latrodectus* in a field in the summer as he slept behind his harvesting machine. He awoke at once and saw an image of a tarantula spirit spider. This victim was hospitalized for a few days until he was judged cured from a medical point of view. When discharged from hospital, however, this farm-worker re-experienced the "bite" at intervals for several years, usually in the same season in the summer, and sought relief in tarantist rituals in which he spoke with St Paul while dancing frenetically.

This potentially direct linkage between *Latrodectus* and tarantism is also evident in Sardinia where the phenomenon existed in the past and has been studied retrospectively by de Martino's protegée, Clara Gallini, and her students. Although the results collected by students with questionnaires are perhaps more problematic than de Martino's own data in Apulia, it seems clear that in Sardinia *men* working in the fields were the principal figures (77 per cent) in the tarantist cult and that they were actually bitten by *Latrodectus*. Here the

symbolic tarantula is always a female spirit of foreign origin
and classified as unmarried, married, or widowed, engaging in
one of these capacities with the possessed male victim (Gallini
1988).

IV

As the presence of *Latrodectus* without tarantism in the United
States indicates, we should beware of attributing too much
to the causal influence of this spider's bite. However, this
Sardinian evidence does appear to reinforce de Martino's
conclusion, based on his data from Apulia, that "the symbolism of the taranta is thus the autonomous result in the course
of a certain cultural and religious history of real episodes of
latrodectism which are relatively frequent during the summer
work in the fields." Hence, as a total cultural phenomenon,
tarantism "was not reducible to latrodectism but was also not
independent of it, since latrodectism must be considered as an
important historical and existential condition for the genesis
of tarantism" (de Martino 1961: 53). But *Lycosa* rather than
Latrodectus remains in Apulia the actual spider whose bite is
supposed to cause tarantism. Thus the Douglas-type symbolic
explanation here prevails over the materialist explanation (cf.
Hunn 1979).

The characteristics and behavior of *Lycosa*, de Martino
(1961: 60) further suggests, appropriately furnish "a series of
images which are particularly apt to provide a basis for the
obscure pulsations of the unconscious, to the aggression of
the hidden past which turns into the strangeness of the
nervous symptom, to the internal bite which leads to
the search for 'he who bites', to the dream of renewal, of
eroticism and fecundity, in harmony with the season in which
you harvest as much as you have sowed and pay debts contracted on the economic plane as well as on the existential."
This imaginative interpretation of spider symbolism, linking it
to the situations of conflict experienced by those diagnosed as
possessed, has, of course, strong psychoanalytic overtones[1]
taking us beyond our present brief which is simply concerned

with the relation between real and attributed features in spider symbolism in Apulia.

Here, then, we have an interesting situation in which there are two zoological models for the symbolization of the archetypal tarantula. Mainly, apparently, on account of its physical characteristics and the immediate pain of its bite, *Lycosa* has been selected as the ideal template in preference to *Latrodectus*. Despite its toxic bite and the parallel between the symptoms it actually produces and those of tarantism, *Latrodectus* is, mistakenly in biological terms, largely ignored. Nevertheless it contributes its web to the spirit spider's symbolic accoutrements, and the real effects of its bite seem to underlie the whole cultural formation and may (although this would be hard to prove) have the causal force postulated by de Martino. Finally, before returning to the Lele, it should be stressed that the features which are seen in the *Lycosa* tarantula as making it a fitting representation of the spirit spider are all treated as *positively* appropriate (size, aggression, speed, impressive bite). The specific aptness of these characteristics is apparently the basis for drawing the equation between spirit and animal. In what follows I shall argue that the Lele scaly ant-eater (pangolin) is endowed with spiritual force not so much – as Douglas claims – because it is negatively "anomalous" and does not fit in anywhere, but rather because it fits extremely well into several different dimensions which it links together, suggestively, serving as a potent bridging symbol. It is thus, as it were, positively over-endowed, rather than negatively under-endowed as a potential symbolic vehicle.

v

Amongst the Lele, as Douglas recounts, the pangolin cult is the only cult in which an animal is the cult object. This fertility cult is open exclusively to men who have begotten children of both sexes, "Pangolin men" being Lele elders who already belong to the less exclusive Begetters Society (cf. footnote 9). The pangolin, which is referred to as "chief," "because he makes women conceive" (Douglas 1957: 55), is ritually hunted and eaten in a communal fertility feast which will bring "animals in droves" and "babies to women." There are, however, in fact two pangolins – the small pangolin (*Manis tricuspis*) and the large pangolin (*Manis gigantea*). Women may not touch the former, nor eat the latter if they are pregnant – but only the first is the object of "a major cult" (Douglas 1957: 57).

According to Douglas, the pangolin is described by the Lele in terms in which there is no mistaking its anomalous character. They say: "in our forest there is an animal with the body and tail of a fish, covered in scales. It has four little legs and it climbs in the trees." For the Lele, "the pangolin is anomalous in other ways. Unlike other animals, it does not shun men but offers itself patiently to the hunter . . . Furthermore, the pangolin reproduces itself after the human rather than the fish or lizard pattern . . . Lele say that, like humans, it gives birth to one child at a time. This in itself is sufficiently unusual to mark the pangolin out from the rest of the animal creation and cause it to be treated as a special kind of link between humans and animals" (Douglas 1957: 50). The contrast with the excessive procreative success of parents of twins is striking. "Parents of twins are regarded as having been selected by the spirits for a special role, mediating between humans, and animals and spirits. Pangolins perform a corresponding role in the animal sphere" (Douglas 1957: 51).

At the end of her original presentation of the pangolin, Douglas raises the problem of the existence among the Lele of the two pangolins and the ritual predominance of the small pangolin, noting that pangolin cults occur in other parts of the Congo and that "a historical solution" may be required here. In a later publication, she returns *en passant* to the problem, invoking the authority of Jan Vansina to say, in effect, that the small pangolin is more anomalous than the large one (Douglas 1975: 46). If this is zoologically the case (as Douglas implies) we should, presumably, find this reflected in a similar ritual discrimination in favor of the small pangolin in other parts of the Congo where it is paid cult and both varieties of pangolin occur. The facts, however, do not seem to bear this out. Biebuyck (1953) describes the ritual killing and consumption of the pangolin by members of an exclusive association, called *Bwamé*, among the Ba Lega of eastern Congo where pangolins are so sacred they are not directly hunted. Here the pangolin which is praised as being "bigger than an elephant," a "true agnate – child of the earth," is revered as having taught man the art of house roofing, house tops being decorated with leaves arranged like the scales on a pangolin. In this patrilineal society, the pangolin is also identified with the maternal uncle, and the sister's sons play a major role in its sacramental dismemberment for ritual slaughter by the *Bwamé*-society. As befits an animal surrounded by elaborate interdictions, the division of the pangolin's meat is a complex process as it is widely shared and after its consumption the participants purify themselves by bathing because "they have just touched a highly taboo'd animal" (Biebuyck 1953: 924).

The cultic treatment of the pangolin here is not identical to, but parallels that among the Lele. However, in contrast to the Lele focus on the small pangolin (*Manis tricuspis*), here the ritual spotlight is on the large pangolin (*Manis gigantea*).[2] Unfortunately, Biebuyck does not give us any very specific information comparable to Douglas's on how generally the Ba Lega speak of their pangolin (*gigantea*). While, like the two tarantulas, both pangolins are nocturnal in habit (a trait not mentioned by Douglas but likely to be of significance for their spirit connexions), unlike the partly arboreal *Manis tricuspis*, the giant pangolin is terrestrial and can swim. It also has the rather arresting feature of standing erect on its hind legs.[3] Although we do not know at present what part, if any, these distinctive features of *Manis gigantea* play in its ritual precedence among the Ba Lega, neither do we know how they are discounted by the Lele. Nor, of course, do we know how such preferences might be affected by wider differences in culture and social structure, between the matrilineal Lele cultivators on the one hand, and the patrilineal Ba Lega fishermen and hunters on the other. De Heusch, for instance, argues from Biebuyck's material that the larger pangolin (referred to by the Lega as the "elder") is the appropriate focus of attention where (as he claims rather than demonstrates) primogeniture is especially valued. Here, according to him, sociological factors determine pangolin preference. But, amongst the Lele, for reasons de Heusch does not explain, cosmological rather than sociological forces prevail and, with its arboreal (bird-like) character, "the cosmogonic wealth of the small pangolin is obviously greater than that of its bigger counterpart" (de Heusch 1985: 34–7).[4]

Amongst another patrilineal Congolese people, the Komo, who live round and to the south-east of Kisangani, it is again the large pangolin rather than the smaller *tricuspis* that is the focus of ritual interest. Here the giant pangolin is closely associated with the men's major circumcision rituals in this extremely ritualistic culture. The initiators' headdress is explicitly compared to the pangolin's head, the claws are compared both to the rattle-adorned ankles of the initiators (which reproduce the sound made by the scales of *Manis gigantis* as it moves), and to the fly-whisks which they wield. In the manner of Douglas, de Mahieu (1980: 39; 1985: 200) argues that as one of the seven principal, ritually significant animals (the others are the large and little crocodile, antelope, python, parrot, and stork), the "large pangolin is ambiguously placed between the class of fishes and the quadrupeds *and from this fact* [*sic*] constitutes a choice symbol for the rites which effect transitions between age-classes."[5] For reasons that are "difficult to explain," de Mahieu (1985: 204) adds, the little pangolin (*Manis tricuspis*) has no particular symbolic meaning for the Komo and is not subject to ritual interdictions.

Here, interestingly, the large pangolin is *not* linked with the Komo equivalent of the Lele association of men who have produced children (the "begetters") – in whose initiation the symbolically charged animals involved are: the large crocodile, antelope, python, parrot, and stork (de Mahieu 1980: 41). Paired with the small crocodile, the large pangolin is exclusively involved in the male circumcision rites. Here, therefore, the "anomalous" mono-reproductive habits of the pangolin appear to be disregarded by the Komo, who seem rather to associate the scaly ant-eater with male potency more generally and, perhaps as Vansina (personal communication) suggests here and in other Congolese cultures, with "big men."

Although we thus have at the moment only scattered, random information on the ritual priority of these two pangolins in different Congolese cultures (underlining the need for a thorough comparative analysis), we should note that the Lele are not necessarily anomalous in preferring *Manis tricuspis*. This ritual preference is shared by their neighbors, the Bushong. For the Bushong, both pangolins are regarded as symbols of fertility and considered "royal animals," linked with kingship and power, but the stress is again preferentially on *Manis tricuspis* (Vansina 1964: 109–10). Elsewhere in the Congo, and indeed throughout much of sub-Saharan Africa, there are indications that pangolins are often endowed with mystical (often therapeutic) power and thus treated as rather special animals. They are not, however, universally subject to food taboos. In some parts of Africa, they are just good to eat.

VI

From this limited and patchy material on these variable ritual preferences, I think we can conclude that if the basis of the pangolin's ritual salience is its (classificatory) anomalousness, then clearly the small pangolin could hardly be intrinsically *more* anomalous than the large pangolin. Indeed, since evidently either can be selected for cultic preference by different ethnic groups and cultures in the same general region (Congo), it would also seem unlikely that anomalousness is the crucial attribute favoring preferential ritual attention. Indeed, more generally, we may question whether anomalousness is a sufficient and necessary condition for pangolin power. Let us, then, return to look more closely at Douglas's own Lele material. What is it actually that empowers the pangolin? The answer seems quite clear in her data and, paradoxically, in the way in which Douglas herself presents them. The pangolin's scaly body and fish-like tail link it with the aquatic domain where, for the Lele, "fishes, water-animals, and water-plants as well as amphibians – are associated with the spirits and with fertility" (Douglas 1957: 50). At the same time, the link with fertility is given a further twist, as we have seen, by the pangolin's habit of mono-reproduction linking it directly with humankind.[6] According to Douglas, a further link with humans is indicated by the pangolin's practice of not trying to escape when hunted, but curling up into a scaly ball, suggesting that it virtually offers itself up sacrificially to the hunter.[7]

In relation to these specific and positive connexions which make the pangolin's role completely comprehensible, the emphasis Douglas places on the animal's alleged anomalousness seems something of a red herring, and is perhaps a consequence of her interests in the biblical abominations which she weaves into her discussion of the pangolin. The fact that the scaly ant-eater manifestly straddles, and so fruitfully links, such different dimensions as animal-kind, spirits, and humans is not in question. But, in my view, these are better seen as providing a series of positive (if lateral) relationships rather than combining to constitute a mysterious anomaly, demanding solution. Of course, the pangolin *may* seem anomalous to the Lele, but this is not convincingly documented in the evidence presented. Similarly, Douglas offers no evidence at all for her entirely speculative and rather far-fetched assertion that, in their pangolin ritual, Lele initiates "confront the categories on which the whole surrounding culture has been built up . . . and recognise them for the fictive, man-made arbitrary creations that they are" (Douglas 1966: 169–70; see also Douglas 1990 and Willis 1975).

In fact, although Douglas emphasizes anomaly (perhaps influenced by the assumed biblical parallels), her presentation of the mediatory role of the pangolin in Lele ideology is actually rather convincingly contextualized in terms of her discussion of the Lele cosmology. As she says, while Lele associate fish with spirits, fish in themselves do not "bridge the gap between human society and the creatures of the forest." But "pangolins, part fish, part animal, friendly to humans, are apt for a mediatory role" (Douglas 1957: 52). Criticisms of her Lele argument on these contextual grounds thus seem wide of the mark. Douglas's line of thought here has been taken a step further by de Heusch (1964; 1971), who suggests quite reasonably that the pangolins in the Lele forest are the counterparts of the initiated Pangolin Cult Men in the village, an antithesis which he predictably sees as part of that between "Nature" and "Culture."

As has been pointed out elsewhere, however, Douglas's more general treatment of the concept of taxonomic anomaly is highly problematic, not to say flawed, since as a rule taxonomies do not, as she seems to imply, necessarily generate perceived anomalies in an unproblematic way (see, e.g., Bulmer 1967; Needham 1976; Sperber 1976; Ellen 1972), and she does not confront the difficulties posed by the existence of logically different levels and types of anomaly (see Ohnuki-Tierney 1980; 1981). But this takes us beyond the scope of the present discussion. Here I have simply tried to show that, although in the anthropological (and derived sociological) literature, the pangolin has itself ironically become a symbol for anomaly,[8] its actual mystical significance for the Lele does not in fact seem to derive from this negative taxonomic status, but stems rather from its varied, positive and multidimensional properties which link it directly and comprehensively with human, animal, and spirit-kind. Its powers seem to flow from these literally perceived attributes, linking it to several cosmological domains. I think that this is also probably broadly true for the other African cultures where the pangolin is treated as ritually powerful. All this, of course, refers to pangolins in general and does not discriminate, as the Lele and some other peoples evidently do, between the small and large pangolin. Unlike the position in tarantism as regards the distinction between *Lycosa* and *Latrodectus*, here *both* pangolins are acknowledged by the Lele as sacred, spirit animals, but with major cult activity reserved to the small pangolin. The Ba Lega in the eastern Congo also regard both pangolins as sacred, but reverse the order of ritual precedence. For their part, the Komo revere only the large pangolin, discounting *Manis tricuspis* altogether. The Bushong, in turn, have the same pangolin preferences as the Lele.

Beyond the fact, as I would argue, that the pangolin offers a powerful generic bridging, or conjunctive, symbol, what can we make of these contrasting cultural preferences? I would suggest that the preferential emphasis placed by the Lele on *Manis tricuspis* may reflect the importance of the "forest" in Lele cosmology (cf. Douglas 1954; 1963), since *tricuspis* is arboreal. This would seem also to explain the similar *tricuspis* preference of the neighboring Bushong (cf. Vansina, personal communication). The Komo, in contrast, pair their ritually powerful pangolin with the crocodile, linking it also with fish, and thus appear to associate it more strongly with the water than with the wooded forest. Hence, if this argument is correct, they select the non-arboreal *Manis gigantea* for special attention. The parallel Lega preference, linked with the ritual significance of the crocodile and a local fish species, suggests that the Lega follow the Komo in emphasizing the pangolin's association with water: hence they also place greater emphasis on the non-arboreal *gigantea* – which can swim – than on the tree-climbing *tricuspis*. These differences, in turn, seem to reflect varying weightings in these cultures' cosmologies between forest and water as spirit abodes. These hypotheses can, of course, only be properly tested by more detailed empirical research. Here, as in the case of the two tarantula spiders, such work would exploit the opportunities for enhanced insight into the symbolization process afforded by the parallel existence of two (or more) potentially appropriate members of the same zoological family.

More immediately, a further comment on Douglas's ideas seems in order. Writing later and more theoretically, Douglas (1975: 306ff.) attempts to develop the concepts of negative and positive anomaly, and claims to find correlations between these and social structure. Thus, she contrasts the negative animal abominations of the ancient Israelites with the Lele pangolin. The former, negative evaluation correlates, she asserts, with a generally negative view of exchange, evidenced in the Israelite stress on endogamy. The Lele, who have a positive view of external exchange and practise exogamy, *consequently* treat the pangolin as a positive anomaly. Whatever may be thought of the Old Testament evidence, the linkage postulated here between exogamy and positive pangolin power is *not* borne out by the data on the Ba Lega whose clans are *not* exogamous (Biebuyck 1953: 903). Moreover the character of Lele social structure itself is, on this point, somewhat problematic. De Heusch (1971: 62ff.) who has elegantly re-analyzed Douglas's material, contends that Lele villages, which are the principal social units, are in fact endogamous.[9]

Finally, there is the difficulty posed by the claim that, on account of their alleged open-armed approach to exchange (however problematic their "exogamy"), Lele have a generally positive attitude towards "anomalies." This might seem to fit the Lele pangolin (primarily, of course, *Manis tricuspis*) but it certainly does not fit such evidently negative anomalies as the "baboon, the scaly tail, the tortoise and other animal anomalies [which] are to the Lele as the camel, the hare and the rock badger to the ancient Hebrews" (Douglas 1957: 50). Douglas does not explain why, according to her interpretation, the pangolin should be so favored, while these other Lele animal "anomalies" fail to enjoy the benefits she attributes to Lele endogamy.[10]

CHAPTER 3

Possession cults in context

I

Anthropologists, no less than the people they study, are much given to the elaboration of those traditions by which men everywhere seek to justify their current interests and activities in terms of some mystically hallowed past. Malinowski himself was among the first to explore the sociological implications of such "mythological charters," as he called them. My own "charter," in this chapter, is brief. My first point is that it seems to me, as to some of my colleagues, that many of the present impasses in our subject, which result from a too rigid adherence to the teleological mystique of status quo maintenance of Radcliffe-Brown (and his "structural Marxist" perpetuators), may be resolved by taking a view of the working of social institutions that owes more to Malinowski and that is essentially flexible, adaptive, and utilitarian. This is the sort of functionalism I hope to deploy here. Second, my subject matter concerns religion and sex, topics that certainly engaged the serious attention of Malinowski and led to the production of some of his most inspired and most popular works. Spirit-possession, or at least those aspects with which I shall be concerned here, embodies both themes. I would only add that, from the tendentious aridity of current kinship controversy and the mechanical, if lofty, metaphysic of Lévi-Strauss, this is a subject to which I turn with a distinct sense of relief. At least the phenomena that we shall examine here have some discernible relation to empirical reality.

Spirit-possession, from one point of view the root of mysticism, is, one need scarcely be reminded, a vast subject. As well as the familiars of a host of less well-known and anonymous shamans, it embraces within a single frame of reference such well-established figures as the Holy Ghost and "Katie King," the controversial materialization produced by the famous English medium Florence Cook and investigated and vouched for by no lesser a person than Sir William Crookes, president of the Royal Society from 1913 to 1915. Lest this conjunction seem unduly forced, let me add that for some theological writers, and not least for the Reverend J. D. Pearce-Higgins, a prominent member of the Churches' Fellowship for Psychical Studies, Katie King's activities have been seen as providing corroborative evidence for scientific belief in the Resurrection of Jesus Christ (Pearce-Higgins 1957: 38).

Our topic includes such other spectacular features as dervish dancing, fire walking, sword eating, and transvestism – to say nothing of such arcane phenomena as "automatic writing." In the realm of ideas and emotions, we are at once confronted by such contradictory themes as innovative inspiration and conservative resignation expressed in catharsis; by aggressive messianic cults and by established religions based on the conservative cult of a supreme spiritual deity.

Spirit-possession thus occupies a central position in comparative religion and theology, in religious phenomenology, in the sociology of religion, and in psychology. With such a vast canvas, I can scarcely hope in a short space to do more than daub a rough outline of my subject. Certainly I cannot do anything like justice to its formidable literature.[1] I shall, however, try to draw attention to certain neglected aspects of the subject that seem to me of crucial importance in appreciating its sociological significance. These concern what in medical parlance would be called the epidemiology of possession, by which in this context I mean the examination of the categories of persons who are most readily prone to possession in different societies. This, I hope to show, is sociologically an illuminating approach and an almost completely novel one, strange though that claim may sound. The majority of writers on spirit-possession, as even a cursory glance at the literature will reveal, have been fascinated by the richly dramatic aspects of possession, enthralled by the most bizarre and exotic shamanistic exercises, and absorbed in controversies concerning the truth or falsity of trance states. In short, their main interest has been in everything pertaining to spirit-possession that, in the idiom of one of the Malinowski Lectures (Beattie 1966), could be termed "expressive."

Such sociological analysis as has been offered has focused primarily on the social roles and statuses of the chronically possessed – whether these be identified as mediums, shamans, or prophets. This position is neatly summed up in Mircea Eliade's book *Le chamanisme* (1951), which is still the standard compendium on the subject. Eliade writes of what he considers the sociologist's proper concern with spirit-possession as follows: "The sociologist is preoccupied with the social functions of the shaman, of the priest, of the magician: He will study the origin of mystical prestige, its role in the articulation of society, the relations between religious chiefs and political chiefs" (Eliade 1951: 8, my translation).

Eliade himself is primarily interested in the metaphysical implications of shamanism as a technique for the attainment of ecstasy in the course of which the shaman makes mystical voyages to heaven and mystical descents to hell. In its "true sense" all this is bound up with the cult of a supreme celestial being. Thus spirit-possession is not for Eliade an essential or intrinsic element but one that is incidental to the shaman's ecstatic mystical flights and his communion with supreme celestial beings.

This conclusion seems to me highly debatable. But whatever may be thought of it, Eliade's program for sociology represents a fair statement of what social anthropologists and others have written on spirit-possession in the past. This concentration of interest on the social roles performed only by those who through regularly recurrent possession and dramatic rituals function as mediums or shamans stands in sharp contrast to the prevailing emphasis in anthropological studies of magic, witchcraft and sorcery. There the trend established by the pioneering works of Evans-Pritchard (1937), Kluckhohn (1944), and Marwick (1952) has been to examine in detail the social nexus in which jealousies, enmities, and frustrations between rivals are transmuted into accusations of witchcraft and sorcery. The ritual and magical acts of witch doctors and sorcerers receive due attention but do not dominate the stage to the exclusion of the relevant social tensions, which must figure prominently in any satisfactory epidemiological approach, and which have been so sadly neglected in most studies of spirit-possession.

This striking difference in analytical emphasis results partly, no doubt, from the dramatic aspects of spirit-possession that so readily seize the attention of the investigator and deflect interest away from any detailed examination of the categories of persons most prone to be selected as mediums by spirits. After all, despite their attitudes toward witchcraft and sorcery, many anthropologists seem to believe in spirit-possession, or at least in some of the powers attributed to those possessed by spirits.[2] Thus much of the literature is taken up, as I have said, with discussion of the psychological status of trance states and the extent to which shamanistic healing rites possess genuine therapeutic value. Even atheists often believe in extrasensory perception. Generally, anthropological writing on witchcraft shows no such preoccupation: there, all is delusion and fantasy.

Such considerations go far, I think, toward explaining this distinct difference of emphasis in anthropological studies in the two fields. But whether they do or not, what I shall now try to demonstrate is that the sort of sociological approach that is now taken for granted in the analysis of witchcraft and sorcery is equally revealing when applied to spirit-possession. This approach has the additional merit of bringing what has too often been regarded as an esoteric oddity squarely into the larger field of the sociological study of mystical phenomena and of religion in general.

II

Little attention, I have asserted, has so far been paid to the question of what categories of persons most frequently succumb to spirit-possession and figure most prominently in possession cults. Nevertheless, the literature is studded with references to the frequent prominence of women in these cults; and some explicit attempts have been made to explain, or at least to comment on, this sexual bias on the part of spirits. Thus W. V. Ivens notes that among the Melanesians of the southeast Solomon Islands, although women are rigorously excluded from the "greater" religious ceremonies, they have a share in the offering of the first fruits, and on other occasions become possessed and may divine and intercede for the sick (Ivens 1927: 472). Similarly, Hogbin notes how in Polynesia women are frequently the mediums consulted for those diseases ascribed to possession by the spirits of the ancestors, thus involving a combination of patrilineal and matrilineal ancestral power (Hogbin 1934: 144ff.). With more detail and sophistication, Fortune shows how among the Manus of New Guinea, while women are, as he puts it, "spiritually disenfranchised in the [paternal] Sir Ghost cult, they are spiritually enfranchised in the *tandritanitani* cults" (Fortune 1935: 95). This statement refers to the mystical power of cursing and blessing, the ability to control the sex of children, and family planning – all vested in the matrilineal line. Moreover, while the morally significant patrilineal ghost cult is controlled by men, it is women who consecrate male diviners and practice as mediums. Here there is a complicated interplay between men's and women's roles that corresponds, to some extent, to the character of the descent system among the Manus, any further discussion of which would take us outside the scope of the present argument.

In the same vein, A. J. A. Elliott in his detailed study of Chinese spirit-possession cults in Singapore notes how, as among the Manus, women are the principal mediums in the raising of the souls of the dead, though not necessarily in the wider practice of spirit mediumship. Yet although in the wider cult it is not only women who act as mediums, it is women who provide the main clientele (Elliott 1955: 71, 134ff.). And in Africa, among the matrilineal Luvale of western Zambia, C. M. N. White has shown the prominent part played by women as the victims of illnesses attributed to possession by their matrilineal ancestors (White 1961: 48ff.).[3]

Again, in that magnificent record of the life of an old Hausa woman, Baba of Karo, the very marked absorption of women in the cult of *bori* spirits elicits the comment from Mary Smith that in this male-dominated Muslim society the "inability of the Hausa women to participate adequately in the ceremonial and public life of Islam leaves a gap which is filled by the spirit-possession cult" (Mary Smith 1954: 271).

These and similar comments by many other observers of such cults, which it would be tedious to cite further at this point, typify the line of interpretation that views the prominent role of women in spirit-possession as a compensation for their exclusion and lack of authority in other spheres. A similar cross-sexual element is apparent in the imagery and ritual drama of possession ceremonies. For whether it is men or women who are the victims of possession – and, of course, I am not claiming that it is only women who are thus affected – the intrusive familiar is frequently of the sex opposite to that of the host. With this high incidence of the possession of men by female spirits, and of women by male spirits, it is scarcely surprising that the relationship between a medium and his or her attendant familiar should regularly be expressed in terms of marriage. Indeed, in many spirit mediumship cults, full introduction into the coterie of the chronically possessed is accompanied by marriage ceremonies and gifts that parallel those of mortal unions. Thus in the flamboyant *zar* cult in Ethiopia the new acolyte is referred to as a "bride" and is assigned two human protectors or "best men." These in ordinary marriages may assist the husband to deflower his bride, and subsequently act as her supporters in all disputes between the wife and her husband (Messing 1959: 437). In the same vein, when a medium exhibits agitated bodily movements in an ecstatic trance it is a commonplace to regard the possessed woman as having intercourse with her incubus.

The matrimonial theme is, of course, familiar to us from the Roman Catholic religious tradition, in which a nun's final vows bind her in spiritual union to the sacred bridegroom, Christ. In the rather different but equally widespread idiom of the stables, in which the relationship between a woman medium and her spirit is expressed in terms of the familiar riding its "mare," this cross-sexual imagery is equally apparent. The cross-sexual element is also evoked in the ceremonial transvestism that accompanies many possession rituals and has been taken by some earlier students of the subject, notably by Leo Sternberg (1924), as an essential and indeed definitive characteristic of the whole phenomenon.

III

I believe, however, that by adopting the epidemiological approach we can go much farther in interpreting the social implications of spirit-possession. Let me start, in the manner of Malinowski, with a brief exposition of my own Somali field material.[4] The Somali pastoral nomads of northeast Africa are a patrilineal Muslim people. Witchcraft and sorcery, as these phenomena are usually defined, do not figure prominently in Somali ideas of causation. Their main religious life is concerned with the cult of Allah, whom they approach through the mediation of the Prophet Mohammed and a host of more immediate lineage ancestors and other men of real or imputed piety who, as in Roman Catholicism, play a vital role as mediating saints. This public cult is almost exclusively dominated by men, who hold all the main positions of religious authority and prestige. Women in religion are merely passive agents and, as in many other Muslim countries, are excluded from mosques. More generally, women are regarded as weak, submissive creatures, despite the demanding nature of their nomadic life, particularly the arduous herding of flocks of sheep, goats, and the draft camels that carry their tents and effects. Milch camels, by contrast, are the concern of men;

and although women are disadvantageously placed in the inheritance of all forms of property, they are especially excluded from ownership of the camels, which form the joint stock-wealth of groups and represent the standard unit of wealth.

In this male-dominated and highly puritanical culture, spirit-possession, which is regarded as one cause among others of a wide range of illnesses and diseases (ranging from slight malaise to acute organic illness) occurs in four fairly well-defined contexts. The first of those concerns cases of frustrated love or passion and involves emotions that, particularly on the part of men, are not traditionally recognized or overtly acknowledged. If a girl who has been jilted by a boy she loved and who promised privately to marry her exhibits symptoms of extreme lassitude, withdrawal, or even more distinct physical symptoms of illness, her condition is attributed to possession by the object of her affections. Here, as in all other cases in Somaliland, this possession is described most generally by a term that means literally "entering."

This interpretation of the disappointed girl's condition is consistent with the traditional sex morality, from which the concept of romantic attachment is, as I have said, excluded. Only within the last generation has this rigid attitude apparently begun to change; and today the explicit recognition and acceptance of romantic love are a common theme in Somali poetry and popular songs. Reflecting these enlightened views, young Western-educated Somalis today describe such cases as a kind of love sickness. The traditional view, on the other hand, is much more in keeping with that exhibited by seventeenth-century French Catholic ecclesiastics in their treatment of the hysterical Sister Jeanne des Anges, prioress of the convent school of Loudon, and her frustrated infatuation for the notoriously amorous Canon Urbain Grandier. As those who have read Aldous Huxley's lively evocation in *The Devils of Loudon* (1952) will recall, this poor nun's condition was attributed to possession by malevolent spirits, and Grandier was held responsible. He was convicted of witchcraft and burned at the stake in 1634.

In Somalia these matters are dealt with less harshly, and no legal action can be taken against the man involved. But it not only men who are the agents or women the victims in this type of affliction. A youth, forced by the overriding control of his elder kinsman to renounce the girl of his own choosing and impelled to marry another, may, if he evinces similar symptoms of malaise or illness, be regarded as possessed by the true object of his affections.

My own interpretation is virtually the same as that offered by young educated Somalis themselves. In the case of the jilted girl, no other institutionalized means is available to express her outraged feelings. For it is only where a formal engagement has been contracted with the consent of the two parties of kin that a suit can be lodged for breach of promise. Her private emotions and feelings are of little concern in a jural world dominated by men. Illness and the associated care and attention offer her some comfort. In the case of the frustrated youth, the assimilation of his plight to an illness – for which he cannot in Somali theory be held responsible – similarly enables him to draw attention to his unhappiness without openly revealing the unmentionable and totally unmanly emotional attachment of a man to a woman.[5]

While these are both examples of cross-sexual possession of one person by another, the underlying circumstances are those of deprivation, in which no other jurally acceptable and institutionalized means exist to enable the injured party to seek redress. This sort of direct, person-to-person possession has close analogies with the malevolent power of the evil eye attributed to forlorn, neglected old women, to beggars, and to the poor in general. Of the treatment administered to the possessed patient in these cases I shall say here only that, as with Sister Jeanne des Anges, the invading spirit is exorcised by a cleric,[6] in this case a Muslim man of religion.[7]

In the other three contexts of Somali spirit-possession to which I wish to draw attention, the possession illness – with parallel symptoms, real or imagined, ranging from mild hysteria or depression to actual organic injury – is attributed to the "entering" not of a person but of a nature sprite. Here I refer to those anthropomorphic *jinns* that in Somalia, as in other Muslim lands, are held to lurk in every dark and empty corner, poised and ready to strike capriciously and without warning at the unwary passerby. These malevolent sprites are said to be consumed by envy and greed and to be particularly covetous of luxurious clothing, finery, perfume, and dainty goods. They are known generally as *sar* (Ethiopian *zar*), a word that describes both the sprites themselves and the symptoms attributed to them; the afflicted victim is described as having been "entered," "seized," or "possessed" by the *sar*.

These are the agencies to which responsibility is attributed for the bouts of hysteria to which young camel herdsmen are sometimes prone. The circumstances are as follows. The camels, as I have said, are herded by the men, and more specifically by boys and young unmarried youths. In the charge of these young men, the camels form a herding unit separate from the flocks of sheep and goats that are attached to the nomadic hamlets consisting of women, married men, and young children. The latter herding unit has a much more tightly circumscribed cycle of movement than that followed by the free-ranging camels, which even in the driest seasons can go without water for up to twenty days and graze far from any permanent well. Thus the camels and their young attendants live a secluded life of their own, often stationing themselves hundreds of miles from the home hamlet and their women-folk. In the dry seasons, the herdsmen move monotonously back and forth between the pastures and the wells, according to a strict regime dictated by the watering needs of their stock. By any standards their dry-season lot is especially hard and demanding. Constantly harassed by fear of attack from enemy raiders and marauding animals, and frequently short of food and water, they are also deprived of the opportunity to meet and chat with the girls of the hamlets. With no regular means of cooking, their diet consists mainly of the milk of the camels in their care; often they are as famished and exhausted as their stock.

In the wet seasons, when the water requirements of sheep and goats, on the one hand, and of camels, on the other, are more evenly balanced, this dreary picture radically changes. The two herding units now move closer together, and the young camel herdsmen emerge from their dry-season seclusion and privation to the comfort and excitement of camp life. It is on their return to this other, welcoming world, with its prospect of meeting girls of marriageable age, that young herdsmen sometimes develop symptoms of hysteria. This is attributed to possession by *sar* sprites and regarded as a mild and usually temporary form of madness; it is not taken very seriously. The remedy is provided by the mounting of a dance called "beating the *sar*," in which it is essential that girls should participate if the smitten youths are "to recover their senses." The accompanying songs, sung by the boys, often have an implicit sexual content, and the expression "beating the *sar*" is, in modern urban slang at least, a synonym for sexual intercourse. In this traditional pastoral setting, however, the youths must content themselves with catharsis and sublimation. There is no open license on these occasions, and the virginity of girls is carefully guarded until they marry. Today, however, the situation seems to be changing, even in the interior. This type of "possession," I am told, is now often feigned and used by youths as a means of pointing the direction of their affections toward a particular girl, who is thus drawn into the dance. All I wish to emphasize here, however, is the element of deprivation and frustration present in the lives of these young bachelor herdsmen, and its traditional outlet in this institutionalized form of possession.[8]

This brings us to the third context of Somali possession, where we touch on a phenomenon that I believe has the widest significance and correspondences elsewhere. The victim of the malevolent *sar*'s attentions is in this case usually a woman, most often a married woman. The stock epidemiological situation is that of the hard-pressed wife struggling to survive and feed her children in the harsh environment, and liable to some degree of neglect, real or imagined, on the part of her husband. Subject to frequent, sudden, and even prolonged absences by her husband as he pursues his manly pastoral interests and affairs, to the jealousies and tensions of polygyny here not ventilated in accusations of sorcery or witchcraft, and always menaced by the precariousness of marriage in a society where divorce is frequent and particularly easily obtained by men, the Somali married woman's lot offers little stability or security. It is scarcely surprising, therefore, that many women's ailments, whether accompanied by definite physical symptoms or not, should be readily interpreted by them as possession by *sar* spirits demanding luxurious clothes, perfume, and delicate foods from their menfolk. It is only when these costly demands are met, and when all the other expenses involved in the mounting of a cathartic dance ("beating the *sar*"), directed by an expert female shaman, are paid, that the symptoms can be expected to disappear. Even then, relief from the affliction may be only temporary.

Without instancing all the evidence I have collected in such cases, let me simply record that in several of them the onset of this sprite affliction coincided with a husband's opening moves to marry an additional spouse, and that in every example known to me some grudge against her spouse was borne by the woman concerned. It scarcely requires the sophisticated forensic techniques of modern anthropology to discover what is involved here; and, very properly, Somali men draw their own conclusions. What the wives call *sar* possession, their husbands call malingering, and they interpret this affliction as yet another of the deceitful tricks employed by women against men. Men support this charge by alleging that the incidence of the disease is much higher among the wives of the wealthy than among those of the poor. This insinuation women in their turn counter with the sophistry that there are some *sar* sprites that attack the wealthy and others that molest the poor. Despite this sociological view of the situation, men's attitudes are in fact ambivalent: They believe in the existence of these *sar* sprites, but with true Somali pragmatism they become skeptical when their own womenfolk and their own pockets are affected.

Depending on the marital circumstances and the value placed on the wife affected, the usual reaction is for the husband to accept reluctantly one or two bouts of this kind.

But if the affliction becomes chronic, and the wife becomes a more or less regular member of a circle of *sar* devotees, save in exceptional circumstances the husband's patience soon wears thin. If a good thrashing will not do the trick, there is always the threat of divorce; and unless the woman herself desires this (as she may), or is actually psychiatrically ill and cannot control her symptoms, this seems usually to work.

Leaving aside the wider implications of membership in a regular association of female *sar* devotees, the point I want to stress here is that in general this characteristically woman's affliction operates among the Somali as a limited deterrent against the abuses of neglect and deprivation in a conjugal relationship heavily biased in favor of men. In a society that offers them little domestic security and very inadequately protects them otherwise from the pressures and demands of men, women may thus resort to spirit-possession, I am arguing, as a means both of obliquely airing their grievances and of gaining some satisfaction. This way of looking at the phenomenon immediately ranks it with such other modes of mystical retaliation as witchcraft and sorcery practiced in societies with other cultural traditions and cosmologies.

This may seem a big jump. But when the social nexus is fully considered the analogy is, I think, justified, and it may seem more acceptable when it is remembered that in many societies witches in fact perform their dark acts by means of spirit familiars. Thus in many cases there is not only a functional parallel between the effects of spirit-possession and those of witchcraft but also an ideological one. I recognize, of course, that it is not the guilty husband but the aggrieved wife who in the Somali case is mystically afflicted. But, as I shall try to show, this difference between an oblique use of mystical power with, in effect, a self-inflicted injury and the more direct line of attack in witchcraft and sorcery is not so critical as might at first appear.

Finally, I mention briefly the last context of Somali possession affliction. This primarily concerns adult men, and not so much a definable social category of men but, rather, psychologically disturbed individuals who, for one reason or another, experience particular difficulties in bearing the pressures and burdens of their society. Just as men are regarded as of the dominant sex and consequently less vulnerable than women, the spirits possessing these unfortunate individuals are considered to be particularly deadly. Again, since men hold the dominant role in the cult of Islam, it is appropriate that the powers involved here should be regarded not merely as especially dangerous but also as especially religious. They are in fact the spiritual analogues of human Muslim clerics, so I call them "clerical sprites." These clerical sprites, I hasten to add, are not a unique Somali aberration but, on the contrary, belong to a category of spirits well known in other Muslim countries and for the existence of which there is, moreover, scriptural warrant in the Koran.[9]

These four contexts of Somali spirit-possession are connected by the common themes of confinement and frustration, which occur in different ways in all of them. This is perhaps most evident in the case of the aggrieved wives, where, to adopt current phraseology, spirits enter the "sex-war." Now the *sar* culture-complex with this emphasis is not confined to the Somali alone. It exists also in Ethiopia (as *zar*), where it reaches its greatest shamanistic elaboration and where it seems to have originated (Cerulli 1923: 2); and it has spread not only into Somalia but also into the northern Sudan, Egypt, and even the sacred city of Mecca itself (Hurgronje 1931).

Its psychological and dramatic aspects in Ethiopia have been described and analyzed most subtly by the brilliant French surrealist poet and ethnographer Michel Leiris (1958). Further light has been shed on its social significance in that country by the work of an American anthropologist, Simon Messing (1958; 1959). Messing records how wives have used the cult in Somali fashion to extort economic sacrifices from their husbands, threatening a relapse when their demands are ignored. Much the same appears to happen in Egypt; and in Cairo, where the cult is prevalent, a particular shop specializes in the sale of the appropriate costumes and other regalia used in the *zar* ceremonies by the female "brides" of the spirits (Kriss and Kriss-Heinrich 1962). This theme is even more explicitly displayed in the suburbs of Khartoum. A recent account reports that here *zar* spirits possessing wives not only demand gifts, including in one case gold teeth, but may also roundly upbraid the latters' husbands in terms that would not be tolerated in other circumstances (Barclay 1964: 198; see also Constantinides 1977).

IV

These "sex-war" aspects are by no means restricted to the *zar*-complex but occur widely in spirit-possession in a variety of societies and places. I do not pretend to have made an exhaustive search of the literature, but I record a few scattered examples. In African ethnography one of the earliest and best descriptions comes from Lindblom's study of the Akamba of east Africa (Lindblom 1920: 229–40). Here a sharp distinction is drawn between the ancestral spirits, which uphold morality and represent the ongoing interests of their descendants, and other capricious spirits. These latter are typically of neighboring tribes – Masai, Galla, and Wanyika – and include Europeans. They are not worshiped but frequently plague Kamba women, who must then be exorcised. As with possession elsewhere, these afflicted women speak "in tongues" in an obscure jargon; but despite the problems of communication, their demands are quite clear. They seek gifts and attention from their menfolk, usually husbands, each spirit asking for things appropriate to its provenance. Thus Swahili spirits demand embroidered Arab hats; and European spirits, articles of European origin. Women may make use of the cult to force their husbands to buy clothing for them. In a poignant little case history, Lindblom records how a woman with a longing for meat could only gain her husband's consent to the killing of an animal by resort to a possession bout in which her cravings were voiced by the invading spirit. Unfortunately, however, she made the mistake, once her desires were satisfied, of vaunting her successful deceit too openly; she was sent back to her father by her outraged spouse.

Parallel instances are reported from Tanzania, where an

affliction, popularly called "devil's disease" in Swahili, is apt to plague women. Again, the possessing spirit, which manifests its presence by hysterical and other symptoms, demands gifts, some of which reflect its provenance. Treatment is a fairly lengthy business, involving not only the usual costly cathartic dances but also the presence for some time of the therapist within the afflicted woman's family. In this enlightened form of therapy, the sick woman is thus made to feel the center of attention; her husband may even be constrained to modify his behavior toward her (Koritschoner 1936). Again from east Africa, in an extremely interesting study of the Taita of Keyna, Grace Harris (1957) describes a similar women's possession affliction, by spirits other than those of the main, morally endowed, male-dominated cult, that functions in a similar manner to exert pressure on men. Here an important element, present in many of the cathartic rites associated with these spirit afflictions, is the assumption by women of male postures and dress.

Analogous phenomena have been described by several observers among the BaThonga (Junod 1922) and Zulu (Krige 1936: 307; Gluckman 1954) of South Africa; in the case of the Zulu, psychological studies are also available (Lee 1950 and 1969; Loudon 1959). Among Junod's Thonga, women were traditionally afflicted by Zulu and other foreign spirits, and the Zulu women in turn by Thonga devils. In both cases there is the familiar pattern of hysterical and other manifestations, as well as requests for gifts and for the mounting of the cathartic dance paid for by the husband. Among the Zulu today, however, this affliction – known locally as "Bantu disease" and diagnosed by Lee as a form of conversion hysteria – most commonly involves possession by Indian spirits and by the *tokoloshe*, obscene little sprites with thickset bodies and huge penises. All this readily lends itself to straightforward Freudian interpretation, and Lee records cures effected on this basis. My interest here is in the institutionalized role of this Zulu possession cult in the sex-war. In this connection I note in passing Loudon's intriguing observation that the rise of these typically feminine disorders seems to have coincided with the decline of the traditional agricultural fertility rituals in which women exchanged their habitual role of submission for one of dominance. These now-extinct rituals are among those referred to by Gluckman in his Frazer Lecture *Rituals of Rebellion in South-east Africa* (1952).

We turn now to west Africa, where elements similar to those we have been discussing may, I believe, be found in the Songhay cult of *holey* spirits and in the Hausa *bori* culture. For the Songhay, I admit, the evidence is not entirely clear. Jean Rouch (1960: 178ff.) records that possession by these *holey* spirits in this Islamized society is more frequently invoked as an explanation of illness in women than in men, although as in many of the other cases we have been considering, men of low status may also be afflicted. Again, there is a whole family of these sprites, some associated with neighboring peoples (such as the Hausa and Tuareg) and others with animals. A modern addition to this spirit host is that of European sprites, who increasingly appear unbidden at the seances in which women play so important a part. Here there is a well-organized establishment of societies of mediums and shamans, in which the low-caste Sorko fisherfolk play a crucial role, along with the usual dances, gifts, and offerings. There is no explicit indication, however, that the cult offers women the direct means of exerting the pressure on their menfolk that we have discovered elsewhere. Further research, I suggest, may well reveal that it does.

The Hausa *bori* cult, which like that of *zar* has spread northward into north Africa, is a similar though more elaborate affair.[10] Here there is a great pantheon of some two hundred individually named sprites, related in various ways among themselves in a manner reminiscent of the gods of ancient Greece. These *bori*, according to Tremearne (1913), range in descending order of importance from the mighty "king of the *jinns*" (*Sarkin' Aljan*) to a small cluster of sprites known familiarly as the "little spots," which despite their innocent-sounding name are held to be responsible not only for a number of minor ailments but also for smallpox. This *bori* pantheon is thus not merely a census of spiritual forces but equally a medical dictionary, each sprite being connected with a group of symptoms (some of which overlap). Both among the Muslim Hausa in west Africa proper and in its northern extension in Tunisia, Tripolitania, and Egypt, this cult is again predominantly one of women, who are the regular devotees in shamanistic exercises designed to exorcise the grounds of their ailments.

But I believe that we can go farther and bring some elements of this elaborate cult within our particular purview. A search of the scattered literature is not very rewarding; the most suggestive clues are that the evil eye is believed to operate through the agency of *bori* sprites (Tremearne 1914: 179) and that a despised and neglected wife is known as a *bora*, a term that Tremearne (1914: 395) connects with *bori*. I do not know whether this is valid etymology or not. But a more recent observer records that in practice the *bori* cult has two main aspects – one inside the Hausa compound and the other outside.[11] Of these, the latter and wider cult has hitherto received more attention from anthropologists. In the internal domestic cult, which has been neglected, *bori* possession, involving only certain selected spirits of the total pantheon, appears to be used especially by junior co-wives against their senior colleagues and particularly against their husbands; it thus figures prominently in disputes within the polygynous family. Here, as in the other cases we have examined, wives possessed by *bori* exact gifts and economic sacrifices from their husbands and in this fashion press their claims for attention.

Finally, a diligent search of the literature will, I think, yield examples outside Africa of the particular type of mystical sanction we have been discussing. Certainly, as I pointed out earlier, women and persons of other subject categories figure prominently in many spirit cults elsewhere in the world, and not least in our own shamanistic tradition, where the sexual element is certainly by no means absent. One well-established non-African phenomenon that seems to support this argument is found among the polar Eskimos and other Siberian peoples and is usually known as "Arctic hysteria." This is a hysterical affliction mainly affecting women and particularly prevalent during the harsh winter months in northern Greenland. Gussow (1960), who interprets this condition in Freudian terms, considers the hysterical flights to which those affected are prone as unconscious seductive maneuvers and invitations to male pursuit. They are, he argues, the refuge of those women who in hardship and crisis seek loving reassurance. Stripped of its Freudian cadences, this interpretation suggests my own line of analysis. It is, moreover, particularly significant in this connection that this hysterical condition, which is generally attributed to spirit-possession, plays a vital part in the selection, training, and ritual performances of Siberian shamans – who are frequently women (Czaplicka 1914: 169ff., 309–25).[12] More recent studies (e.g., Basilov 1981) argue that over the last few decades, with increasing secularization in the Soviet Union, shamanism has been marginalized and has become almost exclusively the province of women.

v

It must now be clear, I think, that we are concerned here with a widespread use of spirit-possession, by means of which women and other depressed categories exert mystical pressures on their superiors in circumstances of deprivation and frustration when few other sanctions are available to them. Of course, spirit-possession is only one possible mystical mode, and one that operates obliquely in the sense that it is the aggrieved party who submits to the affliction rather than seeking to inflict illness on the real source of injury and deprivation. Witchcraft and sorcery are from this point of view other, more direct processes of retaliation and attack; and I do not attempt to determine why in certain societies one mode is favored rather than another – or indeed why in some cases both are found. It may be worth noting, however, that one specific characteristic of spirit-possession is that, unlike at least some forms of witchcraft and sorcery, it appears usually to offer an explanation only of illness. It does not generally explain external misfortunes, at least not directly, and this

seems to follow logically from the specific nature of possession
as an invasion of the person.

Whether or not this will turn out to be a valid and significant distinction, there are important analogies between the
two types of mystical sanction – spirit-possession, and witchcraft and sorcery – to which I have already referred and would
like now to press further. It seems to me that in Nadel's
analysis of Nupe witchcraft, for instance, we find a kind of
witchcraft converse to the enlistment by women of spirits in
the "sex-war" that has been our main theme so far. For here,
through their enterprise in trade and commerce, which often
makes their husbands financially indebted to them, it is
women who get out of hand and cannot be brought to heel
except by accusing them of being witches (Nadel 1952). One
further point in this regard seems worth making. The best
anthropological analysts of witchcraft and sorcery strongly
emphasize the nexus of conflict between the bewitched or
ensorceled victim and the witch or sorcerer. They tend to
forget, however, that in pointing the finger of accusation at
the witch or sorcerer, the victim also draws attention to
himself (or herself). This, I suggest, has the effect not merely
of marshaling public opinion behind the victim in the manner
of the typical witch hunt but also of making the victim the
center of special care and consideration. This, at least, seems
to be a common effect of the whole process, one that has been
singularly neglected in witchcraft analysis. (These issues are
pursued further in Chapter 4.)

In so far emphasizing the sanction and control aspect of the
use of spirit-possession by women against men, I am not
forgetting that other line of interpretation which sees in such
phenomena the assertion of the interdependence of the sexes
and the conservation of the existing pattern of relations
between them. This is the main emphasis of Gluckman's
Rituals of Rebellion, which reflects the traditional structural
approach of Radcliffe-Brown. Thus for Gluckman such
conflicts *really* represent disguised conservation and stability.
This is also the main focus in Grace Harris's interpretation of
the Taita women's possession cults to which I referred earlier.

She, like Gluckman, in the latter's terminology sees depressed women not as suffragettes but as passive subjects, bravely shouldering their man-imposed burdens and only periodically reacting against them in a cathartic ritual acceptance of the established order. In a similar vein, Werbner (1964) has offered an elaborate analysis of Kalanga Shona women's spirit-possession. Although he does show how women use their powers to generate pressures, Werbner argues (if I have understood him correctly) that this in the end is to the profit of men. Here, however, the cult in question is much more central to the upholding of the traditional tribal morality than are the peripheral cults from which I have drawn my conclusions about the special role of women's possession.

In any case, I believe that the material I have so far presented on these peripheral cults supports my emphasis which is less on the conservative, status quo maintaining aspects than on the dynamic role of the mystical sanctions in the war between the sexes. In short, my argument is that if in these traditionally male-dominated societies women are not always actually 'feminists', they can readily become so when the circumstances are appropriate. I now refer for supporting evidence to a penetrating study by Elizabeth Colson (1969) of the Tonga of Zambia. By contrasting the conservative, traditionalist, valley Tonga with their more sophisticated and acculturated plateau countrymen, and using historical evidence, Colson's material reveals what really is at stake in these women's deprivation cults.

Among the plateau Tonga, who have been increasingly involved in the modern market economy of Zambia since the 1930s, and who have local opportunities for earning cash wages that do not require their menfolk to work extensively as absent migrant laborers, there has been a virtually parallel acculturation of men and women. Moreover, the traditional pattern of relations between the sexes is one of equality rather than inequality (Colson 1958: 137). Thus, like men, whether unmarried or married, women participate freely in social activities and are not strongly hedged about with mystical or other constraints. In this situation possession by peripheral *masabe* spirits is today rare, and in so far as it exists affects men and women equally.

Among the valley Tonga the situation is altogether different. Here men have long participated through labor migration in the wider European-oriented world, while women have remained at home, fascinated by the town delights and mysteries but excluded from them. It is these secluded and excluded wives who are regularly subject to possession by spirits, which today characteristically demand gifts that these women associate with their alluring urban counterparts – gay cloths, luxury foods, or (one of the commonest demands of the spirits) soap. This demand for soap reflects a growing male sophistication, a repugnance for the traditional oil and ochre cosmetics applied by valley women, a preference for freshly bathed and fragrantly scented partners. It is in this cosmetic idiom that, through their possessing spirits, these rural women today call attention to their exclusion and neglect and seek to overcome it. In the past, their spirits desired men's garments and possessions.

Thus it is that these women's deprivation cults mirror the changing interests and desires of those who succumb to possession. These ambitions and longings are no longer static, if they ever truly were, and thus cannot be completely contained or explained in the repetitive idiom of ritual rebellion. Equally, the changing character and imagery of the possessing spirits mirrors changing circumstances. To the foreign tribal and animal sprites everywhere so prominent in these traditional spirit pantheons are now added, while they are still novel and mysterious, such other alien powers as those manifest in airplanes and trains. Much the same occurs with spiritual forces of Christian mission origin, which are equally readily assimilated into these peripheral women's cults. With these new accretions, reflecting new contacts and new experiences, some of the old spirits disappear.

Thus, contrasting the record of these cults among the valley Tonga with the position on the plateau, it is clear how in the former case much of the traditional inequality between the sexes continues and so the cults continue, with modifications in the cast of invading spirits corresponding to changing experience of the world. For the plateau Tonga, with their more liberal treatment of women, such possession of this type as exists continues to affect men and women equally. This makes sense only if we acknowledge the at least potential dynamism which I have stressed in these cults.[13]

Now let us take up a different but related theme. I have several times called attention to the fact that the cults with which we are mainly concerned here are peripheral in the sense that they do not embody the main moral code of the societies in which they occur. Thus, it seems more than merely semantically appropriate that many of the spirits that figure in them should represent and reflect peripheral contact with foreign peoples and tangential exposure to novel experiences. But of much greater relevance to my argument is their special connection with women. For whether or not they may be regarded as pawns in the marriage alliance games that Lévi-Strauss's men play, there is no doubt that in a great many societies, and perhaps most, women are in fact *treated* as peripheral creatures.

This I hasten to add is not some special feature limited to patrilineal societies: the valley Tonga are not patrilineal, nor are many of the examples to which I have referred. Here, I may perhaps be permitted to interpolate, we have again a demonstration of the unimportance, from many points of view, of these traditional descent categories with which anthropologists have so long and so unproductively wrestled in the search for fruitful correlations with other social phenomena. At least some anthropologists[14] now realize that descent is a very shaky peg upon which to hang securely many important social phenomena: That great encrusted heart of traditional anthropology is trembling, or should be.

For the peripherality of women is, irrespective of descent, a general feature of all societies where men hold a secure monopoly on the major power positions and deny their partners effective jural rights. Here, of course, there is an obvious and vital contradiction, since whatever the jural position of women, it is they who are essential to the perpetuation of life and of men. It is they who produce and rear children, playing a major role in their early training and education. Thus the treatment of women as peripheral creatures flatly contradicts their fundamental biological importance and, in social terms, clashes with their deep commitment to a particular society and culture. (This point is elaborated in Ardener 1972.) Hence, if it is in terms of the exclusion of women from social and political life and their jural deprivation in relation to men that we seek to understand their prominence in spirit-possession, we must also recognize that these cults, expressing as they do sexual tensions, are yet allowed to exist by men. Here it seems to me possible that this tolerance by men of the cults, and the ritual license and blessing allowed to women more generally, may reflect a shadowy recognition of the contradiction between the status of women and their commitment to society. Such considerations, naturally, do not fully explain the existence of the cults. Up to a point, as with other mystical explanations of illness, the use of spirit-possession as a way of classifying and treating disease implies ignorance of, disregard for, or dissatisfaction with the explanations of modern medical science. It need hardly be added that it also requires a certain prevalence of illness.

VI

Let me conclude this, as it must seem to some, excessive concentration on female ailments by trying to draw together other strands of the discussion into a wider schema of spirit-possession. Nadel (1946) and many others have drawn attention not merely to the changing, flexible, adaptive character of spirit-possession cults, which we have seen exemplified among the Tonga, but also to their frankly innovative potential, epitomized in the "speaking with tongues" of prophets. Let us note also that not only have we been concentrating on peripheral cults connected with women, but that here and there socially deprived categories of men, and maladjusted individual men, have also slipped in.

Indeed, in the *zar* cult in Ethiopia, as with the *bori* and *holey* cults and others elsewhere, there is evidence of a progressively widening spirit catchment. Not only women, but all the rejected and despised – whether they belong to distinguishable subordinate social categories or, as with Somali men smitten by clerical sprites, represent individual deviants – appear increasingly to be absorbed into such cults. Thus in Ethiopia, where in the past women were the main devotees, ex-slaves and people of servile origin and subordinate status generally now seem to find in chronic possession and regular membership in the cult organization a measure of security and opportunity for the enhancement of their position (Messing 1959: 331). Membership in the *zar* club itself offers some emancipation from frustrating traditional confinements, and one new trend toward upward mobility is also evident – the increasingly exalted rank of the spirits that possess people of low status.

In this connection, and especially with regard to the relief offered to those devotees who are genuinely psychologically disturbed, I do not wish to minimize the positive therapeutic functions seemingly fulfilled by the regular use of cathartic and other expressive techniques in these cults.[15] Where possession is peripheral, of course, one cannot say as Marvin Opler (1959: 112) in effect says of the Indian peyote cult, that it is the mescaline of the masses. But even where such cults play a subsidiary role, there is evidence that – as well as sometimes anticipating Freud in their recognition of unconscious emotions and motivations[16] – many tribal peoples have developed curative techniques in their shamanistic therapy that modern psychotherapy has only recently discovered.

But I am afraid that I am straying from my wider schema or spectrum of possession cults. At one end of such a spectrum lie the phenomena that have been our main concern here. They can be characterized as forms of hysterical possession institutionalized mainly as a means by which women, and sometimes other subject categories, are enabled to protect their interests and prefer their claims and ambitions through occasional rather than chronic affliction. There is little formal elaboration of a regular shamanistic cult as such, and the range of spirits involved may be relatively narrow. Spirit-possession here, as we have found it among the Somali, Kamba, Zulu, and others, has much the same effect as witchcraft and sorcery elsewhere, although it expresses tensions more obliquely.

In the next band of the spectrum, spirit-possession becomes more the regular, stereotyped, and thoroughly institutional-ized mode of entry into a specifically shamanistic cult group, with an organized leadership and following. Still peripheral to the main religious cult in terms of which men's actions are evaluated and the universe interpreted, it appeals primarily to women and to other excluded and subordinate categories, as well as to individual deviants. Here more than in the previous case, where the accent was primarily on exorcism, there is a true and regular cult of spirits that may be highly elaborate and encompass a vast pantheon of powers. This is the situation in Singapore, in Haitian voodoo (Metraux 1959), among the Muslim Hausa, Songhay, and the Muslim and Christian Ethiopians, to say nothing of parallel cults in classical antiquity. In these examples it is primarily through regular membership in the cult organization, with its prominent psychodramatic features, that adherents gain assurance, security, and enhancement of status, even if only vicariously. Although essentially not the bearers of the main morality of the society in which they are found, such cults may have great social as well as psychological importance. Here I refer to much more than the shaman's role as fortune teller, diviner, healer, and mediator, significant though these functions undoubtedly are. Think, for example, of the fascinating though as yet hardly explored social implications of the Hausa *bori* cult, with its emphasis not only on the oldest trade of all, but also upon prosperity in trade in general, and hence its vital mystical connection with the founding and success of market centers, where at the salons of the richly adorned *bori* courtesans, nobles as well as commoners vie for favor in the highly stylized idiom of Hausa praise songs.

Such elaborate possession cults as this next shade into true prophetic movements, where the possessed mediums and shamans not only answer recurring problems within their own cultural tradition, but in response to new stimuli and pressures announce messianic revelations and inaugurate spiritually inspired religions with a new and wider appeal and a strong element of moral teaching. The precipitating circumstances and the salient characteristics of such "religions of the oppressed," as Lanternari calls them, have received a great deal of attention both within and outside the Christian tradition.[17] Thus it is scarcely necessary to enumerate examples, beyond pointing out that these include such embryonic and inchoate forms as anti-witchcraft movements and cargo cults, as well as the messianic cults of Christianity and Islam. What may be of greater significance is how often, and perhaps generally, such religions stress eschatological notions of a morally evaluative afterlife. The moral order is sustained not merely by prosperity and happiness in this life, but more significantly by the conferment of these rewards in heaven.

Finally, there are those thoroughly established religions where such a central messianic revelation of moral teaching has shrunk to the proportions of a mere myth of creation and of the origins of man's misery. Here, religion has been so completely assimilated into social life, and so firmly embedded in morality, that the eschatological tradition has lost its savor. Yet such religions are still permeated by the notion of spirit, regularly manifest in their defense of morality and piety through possession afflictions, and undercurrents of the messianic tradition continue in the occasional emergence of revitalizing prophets inveighing against decadence and decay. At this end of the spectrum I am sketching we clearly have the religion of the Old Testament as well as those of the Nuer (Evans-Pritchard 1956) and the Dinka (Lienhardt 1961), where in the convenient paradox of the one and the many, the spirits unequivocally represent man's experience of order and disorder in his universe.

This typological series traces the increasing involvement of prophets in their surrounding social order until their revolutionary fervor is almost completely dissipated. This suggests that the type of religion that celebrates an accepted code of public morality can as readily develop from as precede a messianic tradition. For it seems that in the history of religions it is often possible to trace trends and developments in either direction through the various phases and points of emphasis in our simple schema of spirit-possession and inspiration. And it is also perhaps necessary to stress, obvious though it is, that to varying degrees several of the phases we have distinguished may in fact coexist within a particular religious system at any given time. Thus, to take a very simple example, although the principal emphasis in Somalia is on the engagement of possession in the "sex-war" in the manner I have described, there is also in that case a less significant but nonetheless coexistent organization of spirit medium coteries.

VII

Without attempting any very strict application of this model to the data discussed here, it may be worthwhile to indicate something more of the wider temporal and circumstantial setting of some of the cults with which we have dealt. Thus as Cerulli argues (1923: 2) the *zar* cult in Ethiopia today may well represent the ancient Cushitic religion centering on a sky-god displaced by Christianity and Islam and relegated to the status of a peripheral cult. In Somalia, however, there is no direct linguistic evidence for this assumption, and the cult there seems more securely regarded as an intrusive element. This certainly is the case with the affliction attributed to clerical sprites, which has only made its appearance within the last generation or so. In Arabia, the northern Sudan, and Egypt, the *zar* cult is likewise intrusive and of scarcely more than a century's standing (cf. Chapter 8). In its own local setting, the *bori* cult is generally regarded as the displaced traditional religion of the pre-Islamic Hausa, and there seems no good reason to dispute this view. In Haiti a rather similar relationship appears to have existed over several centuries between the slave and the later peasant cult of voodoo and of Christianity (Metraux 1959).

It seems probable that such displaced and peripherally relegated cults may provide the kind of institutional and inspirational continuity which, in appropriate historical circumstances, enables new messianic cults to develop and eventually to entrench themselves at the center of religious morality. This surely is one of the principal themes in the history of Christianity; and if the prophets of the Old Testament unquestionably herald Christ's messianic mission, the ultimate entrenchment of this religion in public morality in our own society, and the implicit disregard of eschatology except as a convenient metaphor for sanctioning good conduct, bring the cycle full circle. For the main public cult of nineteenth- and twentieth-century Christianity seems more in the morality-upholding spirit of the Old Testament than in the call-to-salvation spirit of the New Testament. Here we should also note the explicit refutation of the Church's traditional eschatology in the doctrines advanced by modern Christian apologists, who argue that heaven and hell are not realities in the traditional sense but rather existential states of mind.

By way of concluding, I would only add that we should also look more specifically at our own tradition of peripheral spirit-possession. In our religious history, the establishment of the Holy Spirit as the sole orthodox source of divine inspiration automatically disenfranchised other spiritual claims that could not be acceptably authenticated and exposed them to charges of fraud and traffic with the Devil, with consequences that we all know. This is the official view, exposed with characteristic casuistry in the late fifteenth-century *Malleus Maleficarum*, written by the Dominican authorities Kramer and Sprenger, which for at least two centuries seems to have served as the principal ecclesiastical guide on such matters. Although the increasingly liberal treatment by the Church of possession that was assigned to the work of Satan, and the rise of secularism and modern science in the nineteenth century, naturally fostered a widening of skepticism regarding peripheral spirit-possession, the phenomenon did not entirely disappear. Indeed, in the Victorian era, and especially after the challenge to orthodox theology presented by the publication in 1859 of Darwin's *Origin of Species*, a new upsurge of spiritualism claiming and to some extent receiving scientific approval made its appearance. This was the heyday of the Fox sisters and of the celebrated English medium Florence Cook, when as Trevor Hall aptly puts it, "as many heads as tables were being turned and the various interpretations put upon the mysterious dances of the furniture reflected the state of mind of those who advanced them. Spiritualists were certain that the tables moved under the influence of spirits; the clergy thought that this was probably true, but whether these discarnate entities were good or bad, angelic or demonic, was open to question" (Hall 1962: xi).

Although as the sustained current of spiritualist seances and publications indicates, spirit-possession in its traditional guise is, like other marginal practices, by no means defunct today,[18] it can hardly claim the widespread interest and following it attracted among our grandparents. This decline seems to coincide fairly closely with the rise of modern psychology and psychoanalysis. And no one, I fancy, will question that many of the medical symptoms associated with spiritualism in our own past and in traditional societies are now treated on the psychoanalyst's couch. But perhaps this analogy can be pressed further. For at least in psychoanalysis, not only is the mode of entry to the profession broadly similar to that of the shaman's spiritual travail and apprenticeship, but the treatment situation of the patient is implicitly, and increasingly explicitly, psychodynamic in its essential characteristics. Certainly in the functional approach to psychiatric medicine so widely adopted today we have an interpretation of psychosomatic disorders – and according to some practitioners, of more serious mental maladies – that relates the patient's symptoms to his or her personal predicament by the same kind of contextual logic I have followed here.

In suggesting this comparison, I am not of course arguing that all psychological illness can properly be regarded as a response to deprivation, nor am I proposing that the whole of modern psychotherapy be viewed as a deprivation cult. The parallel seems best restricted to the incidence and treatment of the neurotic disorders, and particularly to psychosomatic and hysterical afflictions. Whatever other types of malady may be associated with tribal spirit-possession cults, these stand out as the most widely reported symptoms associated with peripheral possession. If the analogy I am proposing has some substance, it is therefore in this field of mental disorders that we should seek correlations between these afflictions and deprivation. Unfortunately, but not surprisingly in view of the difficulties involved in maintaining common standards of diagnosis, detailed statistical information on the epidemiology of mental illness in Western societies is not readily available. Nevertheless, a number of studies contain suggestive data. In their examination of mental illness in New Haven, Connecticut, Hollingshead and Redlich (1958) found a statistically significant *inverse* relationship between psycho-somatic disorders and hysterical reactions on the one hand, and social class on the other. Disorders in these categories are most prevalent among the most socially deprived sections of the community. More recently, an analysis of diagnoses in neurosis cases from a sample of general practices in England showed an overwhelming predominance of female disorders: The reported ratio of female to male neurotic patients was two to one.[19]

In the present state of confusion in what it has now become fashionable to call transcultural psychology, it would be extremely naive to place too great reliance on such figures or to accept the parallel I have drawn without reservations. All I am suggesting, therefore, is that here is something worth considering further. In thus looking to psychology and psychiatry, as I think anthropologists must increasingly do (at least if we want to know the analogues in our own society of the syndromes that we examine and analyze in other cultures), I realize that I may offend those British colleagues who, what-ever their declared theoretical affiliation, remain in practice faithful to the functionalism of Radcliffe-Brown, who was notoriously ambivalent toward psychology (see Lewis 1977). But lest I be too hastily condemned, let me be more explicit. In the psychologist's explanation of bizarre behavior in terms of unconscious motivation, projection, conversion, and the rest, I do not hope to find a final explanation of socially institutionalized behavior that closes the door to anthropological analysis. On the contrary, all I wish to do is to be able to classify and hold constant a range of similar symptoms which are dealt with in a wide diversity of institutionalized ways in different societies. I do not believe that *social* phenomena such as spirit-possession can be explained in terms of psychiatric illness or the malfunctioning of individual psyches. Nor, as I hope is clear, do I consider that a satisfactory explanation can be found in terms of dietary deficiencies (see Lewis 1983). My approach to the topic (which is no more "psychological" than that customarily adopted in the anthropological analysis of witchcraft and sorcery) assumes that all significant social behavior has an affective (i.e., "psychological") dimension. It is not possible to seek to understand spirit-possession in particular, any more than religion in general, without recognizing and acknowledging this.

CHAPTER 4

Witchcraft within
and without

I

The preceding chapter found it illuminating to examine spirit-possession from the viewpoint of the sociology of witchcraft. This chapter returns the compliment, suggesting that fresh light is shed on witchcraft when it is considered from the perspective we have developed for possession. In fact, as I trust will become plain, the process is mutually enlightening.

This can be seen at once when we turn to that recalcitrant problem in witchcraft studies – the fact that individuals sometimes spontaneously confess to being witches. In west Africa, particularly, it has long been noted that people sometimes voluntarily confess that they are witches and have bewitched others. This phenomenon where accuser and accused are the same person has become known as "introspective witchcraft" (see Field 1960; Ruel 1970) and has proved difficult to analyze within the framework of the standard structural-functionalist "anthropological" social tension theory of witchcraft (which of course is really psychological – see Lewis 1977). This theory assumes that the victim of misfortune seeks relief by accusing an enemy (the "witch") of responsibility for his or her ills. Introspective self-accusations, where accuser and accused are the same person, clearly do not fit easily into this scheme, and thus they constitute a problem.

Drawing on the approach to peripheral spirit-possession introduced in Chapter 3, however, R. W. Wyllie (1973) has developed a convincing analysis of introspective witchcraft in west Africa that is probably applicable elsewhere. In the

75

southern Ghanaian material he discusses, the witch is considered to act involuntarily, impelled against his or her will by the "fire within" (witchcraft) to endanger others. According to Wyllie, "Most of those who engage in self-accusation and confess to witchcraft are women and it is generally believed (and this is supported by their confessions) that their witchcraft, like that of child-witches, is always destructive and anti-social. Their confessions typically involve assertions that they have caused the death or illness of children (usually their own, but sometimes those of their brothers or sisters) by spiritually devouring the life-force or soul (*nkra*) of the victim" (Wyllie 1973: 76). A typical scenario involves an anxious mother obsessed by the witchcraft-urge to harm or kill her own baby.

Treatment (by traditional priests, witch-finders, or prophets) is a prolonged process. Confessions are heard during visits to a shrine at which the patient may be "hospitalized" for a time. Throughout the period of treatment for this particular cultural expression of what is known popularly in England as the "baby-bashing syndrome," the witch is visited regularly by relatives and friends bearing special items of food prescribed by the therapist. The cost of the treatment typically falls most directly on the husband of the witch. The cure, as Wyllie describes it, "involves personal recognition, consideration and attention from her husband and relatives who, through their supportive actions, demonstrate their appreciation of her worth and their desire that she should return to her place as a valued member of the household." Although by voicing destructive impulses toward her children the self-accused woman casts herself in the stereotyped role of "wicked mother," the involuntary character of her misdeeds provides her with immunity from blame. The parallels with our discussion of peripheral spirit-possession are striking and hardly require further elaboration.

It would of course be imprudent to suggest that all cases of witchcraft self-accusation conform to this pattern. But if the full significance and epidemiology of introspective witchcraft will require further research, it is nevertheless evident that this phenomenon constitutes a sort of halfway house between spirit possession and witchcraft that confirms the validity of a common sociological approach to both types of mystical aggression. From this perspective, we see peripheral spirit possession, "introspective" witchcraft and (shall we say) "extrovert" witchcraft and sorcery as responses to affliction that at the same time highlight problems in relationships. Because these varied forms of mystical aggression all explain affliction in terms of strained or broken relationships, we might be well advised, before proceeding further, to consider whether these responses to misfortune are mutually exclusive within a particular culture or society.

Those who approach this question from the direction of cosmology tend to answer it affirmatively. In his reflections on shamanism in the Nuba hills in the Sudan, for example, Nadel (1946: 34) concludes: "The Nyima have no witchcraft. Shamanism absorbs all that is unpredictable and morally indeterminate and saves the conception of an ordered universe from self-contradiction." Other anthropologists maintain similarly that if people believe that spirits can injure them out of pure malevolence, they hardly have need of the concept of an evil witch to fill out their view of the universe (see Mair 1969: 30).

This is an excessively narrow application of functionalist assumptions to cosmology and world view, one very typical of the curious but all too pervasive anthropological assumption that cultures and social systems are so economically and rigidly fashioned as to rule out alternatives, duplication, or repetition. The facts here, in any case, are quite the contrary. In many cultures, both witchcraft and malevolent spirit-possession of the kind discussed here do occur. This is true, for instance, among the Venda, and equally among the Kamba, BaThonga, Lenje, Zulu. Pondo, Valley Tonga, Luo, Lugbara, Banyoro, and Taita – to cite merely a few scattered African examples for which data are readily available. Indeed, the very common association of witchcraft with spirit-familiars – often of the opposite sex to the person possessed – is an obvious indication of the impossibility of regarding these mystical forces as mutually exclusive in any given society or culture. Nor is it necessary to look far afield for striking examples of the coexistence of witchcraft and spirit-possession. Our own sixteenth- and seventeenth-century Christian culture is abundantly rich in examples of witches whose malign power was intimately connected with invasive incubi and succubi.

It is thus evident that in many cultures these two forces coexist and sometimes blend into a hybrid phenomenon, as they do in effect with "introspective" witchcraft. That they should not be mutually exclusive at the level of individual cultures does not, of course, rule out the possibility that they might nevertheless have different implications or occur in contrasting social situations *within* a particular community. This suggests the hypothesis that if peripheral spirit possession and introspective witchcraft are found in similar social contexts and produce similar effects, "extravert" witchcraft (the bewitched victim accusing someone else of witchcraft) might be expected to occur in contrasting social contexts. This seems all the more likely in view of the distinction between possession and introspective witchcraft as *indirect* strategies of attack, on the one hand, and extravert witchcraft accusations as direct aggression on the other.

Table 1, which summarizes conveniently accessible evidence from a number of African cases, appears to confirm that indeed possession and interpersonal witchcraft accusation typically occur in contrasting social contexts. In the examples in the table, involuntary seizure by capricious peripheral spirits seems to be primarily restricted to the domestic domain, where it is employed by female dependents against their menfolk; sometimes, as with the Gurage in Ethiopia, it is also applied by male subordinates to bring pressure to bear upon superiors. Witchcraft and sorcery accusations, by contrast, appear to operate in a wider sphere of interaction and to occur in general contexts of animosity and hostility, particularly between equals, or between superior and subordinate. In those cases where witchcraft accusations are levelled by an inferior against a superior (as with the unpopular

Table 1. *Social contexts of peripheral possession and witchcraft*

People	Context of primary peripheral spirit-affliction is domestic domain, women vs. men	Context of witchcraft (sorcery) is generalized enmity, including that between co-wives
Akamba, Ba Thonga, Lenje, Taita, Ba Venda, Zulu, Valley Tonga, Luo, Banyoro	Yes	Yes
Lugbara	?	Yes
Gurage	Yes*	?

*and subordinate Fuga versus freeborn Gurage men

Lugbara elder), the intention seems to be to question the existing distribution of authority and ultimately to discredit the superior, casting him down from his pedestal and asserting equality. More specifically, in the polygynous family nexus, rivalry between co-wives characteristically takes the form of accusations of witchcraft or sorcery; in conflicts between husband and wife, the latter tends to resort to spirit-possession (or introspective witchcraft), the former to accuse his wife of witchcraft.

I do not claim that these distinctions are absolute, but I think that the evidence indicates trends in these two directions. This suggests that the oblique spirit-possession/ introspective witchcraft strategy attempts to redress a painful situation by making claims for attention and demonstrations of regard from a superior without completely challenging the unequal relationship. It expresses insubordination, but not to the point where it is desired to sever the relationship or subvert it entirely. It ventilates aggression and frustration within the status quo. Witchcraft and sorcery accusations, by contrast, representing as they do a much more direct line of attack, express hostility between equal rivals, or between superior and subordinate (here reflecting the operation of spirit-possession in the reverse direction), and often seek to sunder an unbearably tense relationship (see Marwick 1965: 171–91). Thus, where they occur together in the same culture as alternative strategies, peripheral spirit-possession (or introspective witchcraft) usually offers a milder, less revolutionary line of attack, a less disruptive conflict strategy.

Consistent with these distinctions, possession-afflictions in wives do not normally seem to provide immediate grounds for divorce by the husband, whereas accusations of witchcraft directed against a wife may be used for this purpose. Thus, for example, among the South African Venda, where in the 1930s divorce was rare and not readily obtained, one of the special circumstances in which a wife could be divorced was when she had been designated a witch (Stayt 1931: 152). Again among the Venda, some indication of the relative strength and severity of the two lines of attack is provided by the fact that if peripheral spirit-possession actually led to a possessed woman's death, her husband could accuse his wife's mother of being a witch and demand and receive compensation for the killing (Stayt 1931: 305).

Finally, at the cosmological level also I think we can detect the same regular contrasts between the two types of power. Witchcraft and sorcery are regularly identified with incest, subversion, or even inversion of all commonly accepted moral values. In the popular folk view they represent the negation of morality and of normal social relations. The peripheral spirits with which we are concerned here, however, although also evil, are often not painted quite so black. Above all, they are capricious and mischievous, striking without any cause that can be directly referred to social relations or moral assumptions. In fact they seem to epitomize amorality rather than immorality. They stand completely outside society, inhabiting a world apart from that of men yet in many ways modeled on that of men. They typically range free in nature and are not subject to human constraints. They roam wild in the bush, are disaffiliated, inhuman, come from outside the culture in which they figure as sources of tribulation. All this seems consistent with the other distinctions we have noted between the two modes of mystical attack.

II

So far I have been arguing that where spirit-possession and witchcraft are both found in the same culture they tend to be evoked in different social contexts and to have different social effects, although I admit that the differences may be only of degree. However, in many societies the situation is in reality more complex than this, since the two phenomena frequently merge or coalesce into a hybrid force, at least in some contexts.

Thus for example among the Lugbara in Uganda (Middleton 1969) there are two separate classes of diviners. The first, who are exclusively men and whom Middleton calls oracles, divine sickness caused by the ancestors in punishment of sins. The second, exclusively women or homosexual males, divine in cases of sickness ascribed to witchcraft or sorcery. These latter diviners, unlike their heterosexual male counterparts, are inspired through possession by peripheral spirits. From Middleton's earlier published data it is not clear to me whether spirit-possession also operates in the conjugal context discussed earlier, but it is surely highly significant that here we find spirit-possessed women enlisted as diviners in cases of witchcraft and sorcery that often arise in situations of lineage fission and lead to the erosion of the authority of established leaders (Middleton 1960). Among the Lugbara, such spiritually inspired divination is reported to be a recent innovation. This suggests that it may be interpreted as a kind of spiritual feminist movement having the effect of opening up new and highly significant avenues of social advancement for women.[1]

Whether or not this is a valid interpretation, here we see spirits enlisted in the fight against witches; whether diviners are also sometimes suspected of being themselves witches or sorcerers is not yet clear. However, in a number of other cases this association is definitely present. In Bunyoro, for instance, where it is evident from some of Beattie's case material (1961: 24) that peripheral spirit-possession may act as a restitutive mechanism in the conjugal situation, the same type of possession is also involved in one kind of sorcery and in divination (Beattie 1963: 44–5). Here "professional sorcerers" who sell their services to the public may also be spirit-inspired diviners, and sorcery can be employed either through the use of malevolently powerful *mahembe* horns or through medicines and techniques supplied by mediums possessed by peripheral spirits of foreign origin.[2] These latter "black" spirits seem to be increasing at the expense of the "white" *mbandwa* – the Cwezi "hero-gods" of the former legendary rulers of Bunyoro.

Again, among the Luo of Kenya, where a well-defined peripheral spirit-possession cult connected with women has been clearly described by Michael Whisson (1964), diviners may also be inspired by such spirits both to cure and to cause disease. In this case married women regularly succumb to possession-afflictions, bringing pressure on their husbands and in due course graduating to become spirit-possessed diviners. Those who thus come to control these spirits, however, may also use them in witchcraft against others. Much the same appears to be true in the case of the Lenje described by Earthy (1933: 196ff.), where wives are armed by spirit-possession against their husbands and may also graduate in time to become mistresses of spirits operating both as diviners and as sorcerers (or witches). Male diviners, in contrast, practice in the context of the ancestor cult.

In dealing with this and other similar material it seems useful to distinguish between what might be called a "primary" and a "secondary" phase in the onset and socialization of possession. In the primary stage, women use "involuntary" and uncontrolled possession in the domestic domain as a recurrent means of coping with the stresses and difficulties of matrimony, for which they hold their husbands responsible. These difficulties are alleviated by gifts and special gestures of conciliation and consideration from the husbands. In the secondary phase, such women have graduated through membership in a regular possession coterie or cult group to become controllers of spirits. They now serve as therapists and diviners, thus assuming an active role that readily leads them to be accused of being witches or sorcerers. The factors that lead them into the second phase may relate to a radical change in the domestic situation (such as divorce or bereavement), or to some stage in the developmental cycle of the family. In any event, I suggest that the hostile reactions that primary-phase possession undoubtedly evokes on the part of men come to focus mainly on the secondary phase, in which possessed women, controlling their spirits, assume authoritarian roles that more directly threaten or challenge male authority. Hence the assumption that such diviners may be sorcerers (or witches); hence also the equation, controlled spirit-possession equals divination-sorcery (or witchcraft).

We should immediately add that this transformation of peripheral possession into witchcraft is not limited to repetitive phases within the developmental cycle of families. It may also correspond to socioeconomic changes affecting the relative status of men and women in a developing, and in essence irreversible, historical process. As Susan Reynolds Whyte (1981) points out, what is ultimately taking place here is a dialogue involving male and female discourses about power. This is dramatically reflected in the changing significance of the *avambakali* spirit cult of the Bashu in Zaire (Packard 1980). In the course of radical economic and political changes that have in some ways liberated women at the expense of men, these cannibalistic bush spirits have come to empower female witchcraft directed against men. In this form of mystical attack, *men* are possessed by these witchcraft familiars, which in the course of diagnosis and treatment directly implicate particular aggrieved women. The sanction of witchcraft accusation, however, is in this context by no means an unambiguously effective means of reasserting male dominance.

III

So far we have been concerned with possession by peripheral spirits as a response to tension experienced in different social contexts and its institutionalization in curing and divination by women who are liable to be concurrently suspected of being witches. In other cultures a further pattern of association between witchcraft and possession is evident.

Among the Pondo of South Africa, for example, witchcraft is quite unambiguously connected with possession by evil peripheral spirits. Witches are generally women and are inspired by obscene familiars – the *tokoloshe*, with their grotesquely large penises, through whose malign power they can illegitimately destroy life and property (Hunter 1936: 275–320). The concept of witchcraft here is very close to that prevalent in Europe between the fifteenth and seventeenth centuries – witches inspired by possessing incubi. As in European witchcraft, the possession of such familiars is taken as proof of witchcraft. Among the Pondo, however, it seems that no distinction is made between "primary" possession in the conjugal sphere and witchcraft at large; that is, there is no specialized female possession that can be distinguished from witchcraft and used against husbands in the marital context. Yet women also figure significantly as diviners, fighting witchcraft. In this case, however, they are possessed not by peripheral spirits (= witchcraft), but by the ancestors. Thus an unambiguous conceptual distinction is made between those spirits that animate witchcraft and those that inspire anti-witchcraft diviners, although both roles are generally taken by women. Antisocial malevolence is ascribed to the invasive peripheral spirits that possess witches; diviners owe their power to the ancestors who uphold customary morality. These female diviners thus act as auxiliary functionaries in the Pondo main morality cult of ancestors.

This clear-cut polarity between the sources of witchcraft and afflictions ascribed to its influence on the one hand, and of ancestor-inspired diviners on the other, is fairly closely paralleled among The Gusii (LeVine 1963). Much the same applies generally in Christian Ethiopia (Levine 1965: 68ff.) and in those Philippine communities described by Lieban (1967) where sorcerers are inspired by malign peripheral spirits, and diviners and healers by good spirits that are part of the main morality cult. In this case the cult is that of Latin

Christianity and has not only morphological resemblances but also direct historical links with the older European tradition. Here I would only reiterate that, in its developed form, European witchcraft involved possession by devils, while power to treat the bewitched and to cast forth their satanic spirits lay with clerical exorcists inspired by Christ and the Holy Ghost. In practice, this ideologically rigid polarity was sometimes transcended in those not uncommon cases where exorcising priests themselves fell prey to the devils they sought to exorcise.

Hence there seem to be at least two patterns of connection between witchcraft (or sorcery) and spirit-possession. In the first, possession by peripheral spirits is the cause both of witchcraft and of anti-witchcraft divination and therapy, of affliction and its remedy. In the second, peripheral spirits animate only witchcraft; divination is inspired by powers that directly uphold social morality. The material discussed here suggests that, where peripheral possession has an unsolicited, *uncontrolled*, primary phase (as in the domestic situation), its *controlled* use in divination automatically associates the latter with witchcraft. Since it can be applied for good (divination) as well as for evil purposes (sorcery), there is no need to enlist the main morality powers as alternative sources of divinatory and curative inspiration. Where, however, the possessed person is not regarded as the helpless victim of the spirits but is believed to have solicited their support, and only a *controlled* nexus between possession and peripheral spirits is posited, it becomes necessary to enlist the main morality powers in divination and healing. In the first case, peripheral possession-afflictions are ultimately dealt with by taming and domesticating the spirit, by bringing it under control. When this happens, those who can control spirits and treat the afflicted are automatically suspected of being witches. In the second case, evil peripheral spirit-possession is treated by the exorcism of the afflicting spirit – by casting it out, not by taming it – and this requires the enlistment of superior mystical forces.

Indeed, in order to understand the action taken by the

victim of affliction in securing an advantageous outlet for his distress – either through the medium of spirit-possession, "introspective witchcraft," or by accusing someone else of bewitching him – it may sometimes be more illuminating to discard the culturally grounded expressions "spirit-possession" and "witchcraft" altogether and to think instead in terms of oblique and direct mystical attack.

It may seem strange to speak of the action of the accuser, rather than that of the accused, as "mystical attack." But it is after all the accuser, not the accused witch, who sets the process in motion; and it is certainly the "witch" (the "extravert witch") against whom public opinion is mobilized and who is ultimately the target of social action.

IV

If we adopt this broader analytic framework (which takes a further step along the comparative path, away from Evans-Pritchard's particularistic distinction between "witchcraft" and "sorcery"), it is obvious that witchcraft and witchcraft accusation is not the only mode of direct attack. Cursing also belongs here, and may be morally justified. Thus the contradictory facets of the Lugbara elder's role as legitimate invoker of the ancestor's curse and as suspected witch fall into place, and it becomes easier to understand those other cases of legitimately used "witchcraft" that anthropologists so often ignore or misconstrue (see Harwood 1970). Classic African examples of this situational – positive or negative – definition of what we colloquially call charisma include the Tiv concept of *tsav*, a growth attached to the heart (Bohannon 1957), the Nyakyusa "python power" located in the stomach (Wilson 1951); and the Safwa concept *itonga*, excellently analyzed by Harwood (1970). All these represent mystical powers that the established authorities mobilize positively in the "national interest." But, when those in authority no longer command community support and lose control, these forces are redefined as their malign counterpart – antisocial, egotistical witchcraft.

In larger, centralized states, Wyatt MacGaffey (1970, 1972, 1980) has similarly pointed to the recurrent oscillation in African royal power between the morally approved, and therefore positive, use of mystical force in the "public interest" and its illegitimate abuse for antisocial "private interests" (= witchcraft). As in the earlier discussion of the complex linkage between spirit-possession and witchcraft (introvert and extravert), it is important to stress here the contextual moral relativity and fluidity of these positive and negative powers, especially if they seem completely unrelated phenomenologically. Thus in the Christian syncretist religion of Haitian voodoo, magically charged *points*, linked to deadly zombies, empower ambitious individuals to secure success at the expense of others. These antisocial forces are opposed by the benign family spirits – the "invisibles" (*loas*) which come from Africa, source of all good things. However, when a man dies, his personal store of magic *points* (associated with his achievements or charisma) becomes an ascribed part of the legacy he leaves to his heirs. They thus pass into the family patrimony and, becoming a collective (rather than individual) asset, are automatically transformed into *positive* power as benevolent "invisibles" (Larose 1977). As the context shifts diachronically from individual to communal interest, *cultural* magical artifacts thus become *natural* religion.

Thus we see that one form of "witchcraft" (where "witch" is self-accusing) is linked, in terms of its social implications as an oblique form of mystical attack, with peripheral spirit-possession. But spirit-possession is also linked through the role of the assertive diviner with witchcraft in its classic "extravert" form (where accused and accuser are not the same person). The positive face of the latter is, in turn, legitimate mystical power. Positive charisma, we may say, is the acceptable face of witchcraft, and witchcraft the unacceptable face of charisma[3] – that corrupt power so trenchantly delineated in Lord Acton's famous aphorism.

CHAPTER 5

The cannibal's cauldron

I

As William Arens (1979) has persuasively argued, anthropologists are often remarkably casual and uncritical in their treatment of reports of cannibalism in exotic cultures. Disregarding the usual methodological prerequisite of first-hand observation – enshrined in the Malinowskian fieldwork manifesto – our accounts of cannibalism all too frequently rely on secondhand reports. Such lack of scholarly rigor regularly leads to confusion and conflation of the idea or ideology of cannibalism with its actual practice. Hence, many modern anthropological studies inadvertently tend to entrench and further legitimize deep-seated Eurocentric assumptions concerning the prevalence of cannibalism in tribal societies. Although few of the anthropologists involved here would see it in this light, they thus implicitly maintain the tradition of Freud, who in his magnificent cosmic fable *Totem and Taboo* ([1913]; 1950) casually introduced cannibalism to embellish his theory of primordial incest. In the Freudian version of the Oedipus myth, once liberated by the murder of their tyrannical father the rebellious sons, being "cannibal savages," celebrated the event by *eating* him. The subsequent regularly performed ritual slaughter and eating of the totemic animal, which replaced the murdered father, commemorated and replicated the original act of parricidal cannibalism. According to Freud (1950: 142) these hypothetical events marked the crucial turning point in man's evolutionary development – the "beginning . . . of social organization, of moral restrictions and of religion."

88

In fact, the application of the derogatory label "man-eater" is one of the most widely distributed methods by which the members of one group or community dissociate and distance themselves from outsiders beyond the pale. Cannibalism, however, *pace* Arens (1979: 145ff.), is much more than merely a matter of labeling and stigmatizing disparaged groups and individuals. The ideology of man-eating provides a pregnant cluster of imagery and metaphor to express the exercise and experience of power, domination, and subjection which may be realized in different forms in particular historical and cultural contexts. The appellation "cannibal" is not merely an appropriate term of contempt for uncouth subjects at the bottom of the political hierarchy or on the edge of the civilized world. It may be applied equally appropriately by the victims of oppression to designate their superiors. The designation "cannibal" can thus convey a sense of impotence and desperation and is consequently not always flattering to its user. Again, the term may be employed reciprocally between antagonistic parties of equal status and rank. In this chapter we explore this inherently double-edged imagery, arguing that both in theory and in practice cannibalism ultimately derives its perennial fascination and pervasive evocative power from intimate physical experiences common to all human beings. Although psychoanalytic insights may be helpful here, it is thus unnecessary, *pace* Epstein (1979), to invoke particular childhood traumas or culturally specific child-rearing practices in order to understand the phenomenon.

II

The orthodox anthropological approach to the social dynamics of witchcraft, which we sought to expand in the previous chapter, assumes a disinterested (if not disbelieving) external perspective that concentrates upon the accusation and the *accuser* rather than upon the *accused* witch. In the case of cannibalism, an inadvertent personal experience of the author's – shared with Arens and others – reverses the equation and so provides serendipitous food for thought.

Traveling in the remote Ndembu countryside of western Zambia (then Northern Rhodesia) in the late 1950s, I personally experienced and still vividly recall the suspicion and fear with which lonely African pedestrians responded to offers of lifts in my Land Rover. Their stock reaction was to disappear swiftly into the nearby bush. The explanation for this rather striking avoidance behavior, I discovered, was the assumption, widely prevalent in central Africa at that time, that many Europeans were vampire-men who sucked the blood and ate the flesh of innocent Africans. Similar concepts about cannibalistic Europeans flourished with varying degrees of intensity in east Africa (see Friedland 1960), southern Africa, and in the Congo, where during the Belgian period in Leopoldville the white vampire was known as the "man with the lamp." Around the same time (1958) an unsuspecting European firm in the Belgian Congo marketed canned meat in cans with labels depicting chubby, smiling African babies. The product was not an unqualified success.

A similarly mixed reception greeted the appearance in Northern Rhodesia during this period of cans of cheap meat designed for the local African work force market and labeled "For African Consumption" (see Fraenkel 1959). The ill-fated British plan to form a multiracial Central African Federation joining Northern Rhodesia and Nyasaland (now Malawi) to white-settler dominated Southern Rhodesia (Zimbabwe) had aroused deep and widespread suspicion and alarm among the African population. Africans accustomed to the relatively benign paternalistic colonial administrations of Northern Rhodesia and Nyasaland feared that the proposed federation would involve an extension to their territories of the pattern of white supremacy characteristic at that time of Southern Rhodesia. Since the majority of the population were cultivators, there was particularly acute anxiety that traditional land rights would be endangered by an influx of European farming interests from Southern Rhodesia (Watson 1958; Epstein 1958, 1979). In such an atmosphere of mistrust, and with the failure of African political pressure to prevent the establishment in 1953 of the Federation (doomed to collapse six years later under the weight of African opposition), rumors quickly spread in Northern Rhodesia that the meat marked "For African Consumption" contained human flesh specially doctored to break down African resistance to the unpopular policy of federation. Seeking to counter such fears, a European district commissioner on the Northern Rhodesian copper belt publicly consumed the meat to prove that it was harmless. This demonstration almost certainly had the paradoxical effect of confirming rather than allaying general African fears that Europeans were cannibals. Nor was African public opinion on this issue likely to be disabused by the conviction, about this time, in a European court in Nyasaland, of an African accused of trying to sell two well-fattened children to a European for his Christmas dinner.[1]

In some parts of Africa, as in other European colonies, it appears possible to trace a link between this view of Europeans as cannibalistic blood-suckers and blood donation campaigns. Sometimes these ideas are (or were) associated through the color red, with European-introduced fire services and fire stations (while still novel) acquiring a sinister reputation as centers for extracting and collecting the African blood believed to be consumed by Europeans to sustain their vitality (Friedland 1960). Similarly, in Northern Rhodesia rural health campaigns involving blood tests have sometimes precipitated outbreaks of panic, during which consumption of tinned tomato juice by Europeans has been taken as further proof of their lust for blood. More recently, in southern Africa as a whole, it does not require much imagination to grasp the further medical confirmation of these ideas provided by reports of Dr. Christian Barnard's transplant surgery, utilizing in some cases hearts from African bodies to give new life to whites.

In the more distant past, there is direct evidence that African fears about the vampire propensities of Europeans are also in part a reflection of the slave trade. And it is ironic to note that both the Arabs and the Europeans involved in this traffic appear to have spread rumors accusing each other of practicing cannibalism.[2] Such allegations naturally helped to reinforce and extend the existing indigenous belief in the reality of cannibalism, associating it, in particular, with rapacious invaders.

These factors, however, do not alone suffice to explain how Africans came to suspect Europeans of being cannibals. To understand this fully we have to set cannibalism in context as part of a wider constellation of ideas concerning mystical power in general and witchcraft in particular. It is obviously significant that Europeans were believed by Africans not only to indulge in cannibalism but also to practice witchcraft. From an African perspective, it was largely *because* Europeans were seen as witches that they were liable to be suspected of practicing cannibalism. Witches, as we know, employ sinister forces to achieve selfish ends to the disadvantage of virtuous citizens and neighbors. Success – in the "limited good" witchcraft scenario (cf. Foster 1965) – is at the expense of others. The witch, consequently, inevitably becomes endowed with all the antisocial vices that are the counterparts of corresponding social virtues. Hence the inverted witch stereotype includes all manner of sexual perversion, incest, and the ultimate denial of human sociability and commensality – cannibalism. "Witches eat people," as the Nso of Cameroon (Kaberry 1969), the Shona of Zimbabwe (Crawford 1967), and many other peoples succinctly state. Indeed, the statement, "A witch is a cannibal," is one of the more widely current minimum definitions of the witch role.

Those who define the epitome of evil in this way also believe that the mystical forces that so enable ambitious, unscrupulous individuals to achieve more than their fair share of life's good things can, in other contexts, be used positively in the general interest. As we emphasized in the previous chapter, what anthropologists regularly translate from other cultures by the English term "witchcraft" (or the French *"sorcellerie"*) is, on closer inspection, typically ambiguous. Those whom English anthropologists describe as socially approved "witch doctors" because of their expertise in combating and countering illicit witchcraft usually owe their success to causing what they cure. Here the negative side empowers the positive side which legitimates it. The "python power" of the Nyakyusa (referred to earlier) both provides the basis of witchcraft and empowers the positive righteous indignation of the village elders to defend the local community against external threat. Similarly, as we saw, the mystical force that enables the elders among the Tiv of Nigeria to uphold morality and protect their community is equally the source of malevolent witchcraft. A Tiv witch seeks to obtain selfish aims at the expense of others, and to secure success nourishes his *tsav* on a diet of human flesh – cannibalism again becoming a critical element in the definition of "witch." In precisely the same vein, unpopular Amazonian shamans are denounced as "witches" practicing cannibalism against their own people – aggressive shamanic power in the Amazon generally being associated with the anaconda and jaguar (Lévi-Strauss 1966; Reichel-Dolmatoff 1971; Hugh-Jones 1980; Colajanni 1982; Seymour-Smith 1984).

So too accusations of abuse of power (implying, as we have seen, witchcraft) leveled today against African government ministers and chiefs may include the denunciation "cannibal" (cf. MacCormack 1983). Here we need again recall the equivocal nature of power and its mystical implications. What was typically involved was essentially control over the ruler's subjects and lands, whose fecundity was affected by the chief's mystical energies, which had always to be protected and maintained at the requisite level of effectiveness. In Africa, as elsewhere, leaders were expected to have sex appeal. There was always some connection, however concealed, between such political sexuality and the fertility of people and land. The Bemba of Zambia illustrate these themes with unusual directness. Their kings, members of the ruling clan (whose totem is the man-eating crocodile), were expected regularly to perform ritual sexual intercourse with their wives in order to promote the prosperity of their land and its inhabitants (Richards 1968).

It is against such traditional attitudes toward power (which, as Balandier remarks, is never completely emptied of religious content) that we should understand the conviction, widespread in colonial Africa, that Europeans were cannibalistic witches. The superior military and material technology of the white man, the sources of which were unfamiliar and often mysterious; his miraculous healing medicines; the Christian religion, which underpinned his moral superiority and helped him to maintain law and order in adverse conditions: all these inevitably suggested that the European possessed a unique store of mystical power. If some aspects of European colonial rule were perceived as beneficial, others were not; and here as elsewhere, the exercise of authority always engendered some resentment against the rulers. What is involved here is more complex than simply colonial exploitation.

African suspicions concerning the sinister roots of European power received additional support from the way in which European colonial administrations and missions reacted to traditional African beliefs in witchcraft (and sorcery). Proclaiming that witches did not exist, European administrations had typically made it illegal for Africans to accuse or punish suspected witches. Legislation proscribing witchcraft accusations was introduced throughout British Africa. The Southern Rhodesia Witchcraft Suppression Act of 1899 is a typical example from the region that is our primary focus here. The act is primarily concerned to prevent "imputations" of witchcraft, as the following extracts indicate:

In this Act "witchcraft" includes the "throwing of bones," the use of charms and other means or devices adopted in the practice of sorcery.

Whoever imputes to any other person the use of non-natural means in causing any disease in any person or animal or in causing any injury to any person or property, that is to say, whoever names or indicates any other person as being a wizard or witch shall be guilty of an offence and liable to a fine not exceeding two hundred dollars or to imprisonment for a period not exceeding three years, or to whipping not exceeding twenty lashes or to any two or more of such punishments.

Whoever, having so named and indicated any person as a wizard or witch, is proved at his trial under section three to be by habit and repute a witch doctor or witch finder shall be liable, on conviction, in lieu of the punishment provided by section three to a fine not exceeding five hundred dollars or to imprisonment for a period not exceeding seven years or to whipping not exceeding thirty-six lashes or to any two or more of such punishments.

As Gordon Chavunduka, the first black African professor of sociology at the University of Zimbabwe,[3] observes, the aim of this act is not to punish witches but those who expose witches (by making witchcraft accusations), and consequently in rural Zimbabwe it is regarded today as a "very unjust piece of legislation" (Chavunduka 1980: 130). In a similar fashion, in French Africa, the *Code Penal Indigene* and later the *Code Napoleon* outlawed witchcraft accusations (cf. Alexandre 1974). The effect, of course, of such colonial legislation and its implementation in administrative (and sometimes "native") courts was to *protect* witches and to suppress legitimate means of exposing witchcraft. For those believing in witchcraft the obvious conclusion to draw was that the European rulers were on the side of the witches – and hence, indeed, given all the other aspects of their political superiority, "super-witches." This seems to me the most potent factor in the train of circumstantial evidence leading to the ascription of cannibalistic witchcraft to Europeans (including unsuspecting anthropologists).[4]

IV

It is ironic that those who do not believe in witchcraft should as a result be suspected of practicing it. Cannibalism, on the other hand, is often not practiced by those believed by anthropologists to be cannibals. This strange anthropological paradox, which despite their close connection treated witchcraft and cannibalism so differently, reflects the outright disbelief with which reports of witchcraft are usually received, in contrast to the reception usually accorded reports of cannibalism. The stock anthropological response to the juxtaposition of the two is very revealing. Firmly believing that witchcraft does not exist, anthropologists are likely to dismiss as pure fantasy reports of cannibalism in a witchcraft context. In other contexts, the response to reports of cannibalism is often much less critical.

This intriguing contrast in emphasis and interpretation (paralleling that already noted in Chapter 4 in the treatment of witchcraft and spirit-possession) can be seen in what still remains the most comprehensive and subtle anthropological analysis of witchcraft – Evans-Pritchard's magisterial work on the Azande of the southern Sudan and Congo, to which we have already referred (Chapter 3). If the reality of witchcraft is unacceptable to Evans-Pritchard, there is no question of the reality of accusations of witchcraft, since these can be readily observed and the associated diagnostic rituals and alleviating procedures recorded in minute detail. The famous Zande distinction (to which we have already referred) between "sorcery" as an objective physical technique and "witchcraft" as a psychic force, also happens to accord with Evans-Pritchard's Eurocentric, objective bias. This distinction, in turn, appears to have led Evans-Pritchard to emphasize the unintentional, unpremeditated aspects of Zande witchcraft as an unconscious phenomenon at the expense of the conscious, deliberate aspects that are uppermost in the mind of the bewitched accuser. Although he presents detailed evidence for both these contradictory facets, this at least is how the overall picture of Zande witchcraft has usually been "read";[5] and it is, I suggest, in harmony with the broader distinction between witchcraft and sorcery.

It is not unreasonable to suggest that Evans-Pritchard's own disbelief in witchcraft helps him to investigate with admirable detail and precision the complex issue of Zande skepticism – a topic almost completely ignored in the same author's celebrated account of the theistic beliefs of the Nuer (published after his conversion to the Catholic faith).[6] Confident as he was in discounting the efficacy claimed for witchcraft by the Zande, Evans-Pritchard was more cautious in

his assessment of references to Zande cannibalism. Having
subjected earlier travelers' allegations to devastating and
caustic criticism, he nevertheless felt it imprudent to dismiss
them entirely, on the grounds that "there is no smoke without
fire" (Evans-Pritchard 1965: 153).

Here, as usual, much turns on the accurate rendering of
native statements and so on translation, which, as is well-
known, Evans-Pritchard himself saw as the crux of the
anthropological endeavour. A more recent study of Zande
mystical beliefs by the Austrian anthropologist Manfred
Kremser (1981) sheds important new light on this problem.
Kremser shows that the term *kawa*, translated into English as
"human meat" and usually taken in the Zande literature as
evidence of cannibalism, relates primarily to the witchcraft
domain. Thus the witch may attack his victim by extracting
the latter's life force (*kawa*), putting it in a pot, and typically
hanging the pot with its contents on a tree. This is a state
of raw suspense. For if this *kawa* is cooked and eaten, the
bewitched victim can never recover. If, however, events do not
proceed to this irreversible conclusion and the *kawa* remains
uncooked and unconsumed, the witch can be persuaded to
unbind this life essence from the branch and restore it to the
bewitched victim, who is then expected to recover. Curiously,
as far as I have been able to determine, Evans-Pritchard's
richly documented study of Zande witchcraft does not
contain any mention of *kawa* and does not explore this
important relationship between the process of witchcraft
attack (which he refers to as "vampirism") and cannibalism.
This specific linkage, however, is clearly present in a text
which in Evans-Pritchard's translation (1937: 35) includes the
following passage: "Witches arise and beat their drum of
witchcraft. The membrane of this drum is human skin . . .
Their drum call is 'human flesh, human flesh, human flesh.'"
Although Evans-Pritchard does not tell us this, it would
thus appear that *one* of the sources for the imputation of
cannibalism to the Zande rests on the (metaphysical or
psychic) consumption of "human flesh" extracted from their
victims by witches.

v

More generally, this contrasting anthropological treatment of witchcraft and cannibalism, and the ironical readiness on the part of some anthropologists to view as cannibals those who are prone to view Europeans in the same light, cannot of course be explained in quite the same terms as our central African examples. We can understand the anthropological disbelief in witchcraft more easily than the anthropological belief in cannibalism. The functionalist William Arens (1979: 184), appropriately enough, has proposed a functionalist explanation for his colleagues' lingering credulity. The appellation *cannibal*, he argues, continues to have wide exotic appeal. As the study of cannibals, anthropology is thereby made to seem more exciting. At the same time, anthropologists have a professional interest in maintaining their uniquely privileged role as the specially licensed mediators between their Western world and the exotic alien cultures which, through the imputed stigma of cannibalism, help define the boundaries of Western civilization.

I do not dissent at all from this view of the exploitative, entrepreneurial role of anthropology and anthropologists (cf. Lewis 1976: 34). But to claim, as Arens does, that in general the concept "cannibal" primarily functions as a boundary marker or label distinguishing "us" (non-cannibals) from "them" (cannibals) hardly does justice to the relevant data. The suggestion (Arens 1979: 145) that groups of similar culture have *more* need to resort to the distancing (not-us) label "cannibal" is interesting, but not substantiated – and in fact appears unconvincing. Arens seems also to imagine that since witchcraft does not exist (except as a reality of thought) the same applies to the linked concept of cannibalism, which must therefore be accorded the same mythical status.[7] This perspective on cannibalism is clearly biased in the direction of the negative aspects of witchcraft and takes little or no account of mystical ambivalence or positive charisma. To reach a more balanced and comprehensive view, we must acknowledge that when people interpret the actions of others in terms of cannibalism, they are making statements of more pervasive significance than mere intellectual labeling. As Sahlins (1983: 88) cogently puts it: "Cannibalism is always 'symbolic' even when it is real." To proceed further, we should, I believe, pay close attention to body symbolism, recognizing the extent to which the biological functions of the human body provide a fertile matrix for potently charged ("natural") symbols.

In applying this perspective to cannibalism we should begin by noting that its most general cultural context – either as idea or as actual practice – is usually a ritual setting. Here, where a tabooed negative action – eating human flesh – acquires positive force, the ritual consumption of parts of the human body enables the consumer to acquire something of the body's vital energy. Ritual cannibalism (as indeed Arens himself recognizes) is consequently a form of sacrificial communion. Indeed, it is perhaps *the* prototype of sacrificial communion, since as Sahlins[8] maintains (no doubt correctly) "cannibalism exists *in nuce* in most sacrifice." As is well-known, this has very powerful resonance in the Christian Eucharist, where according to the official doctrine communicants consume the bread and wine that through the miracle of transubstantiation becomes the flesh and blood of Christ. The case of cannibal converts to Christianity is thus particularly poignant, as Sahlins, referring to nineteenth-century missionary accounts in the Marquesas, trenchantly observes.

The Trobriand Islanders practiced a more direct and lurid form of commemorative cannibalism than the Eucharist (Malinowski 1929: 133). The body of a deceased man was exhumed and dismembered by his sons and other (nonmatrilineal) relatives. Although, as Malinowski observed, the mourners found this extremely repugnant, they were expected to display their filial piety by sucking the decaying flesh of the corpse they were dismembering. The bones were conserved as relics commemorating the dead, reverently wrapped in dry leaves, and finally deposited on rocky shelves overlooking the sea. With subtle changes of symbolic emphasis, similar practices are reported elsewhere in

Melanesia. Until as recently as 1950, for example, the Gimi of
the New Guinea highlands practiced what might be called
compassionate cannibalism. Women were expected to eat
the dead bodies of their men in order to release the latters'
individual spirits, freeing them to rejoin the collective body
of ancestral forest spirits. According to Andrew Strathern
(1982: 125), as they ate the men's bodies women used to sing
seductively, "Come to me lest your body rot in the ground.
Better it should dissolve inside me." There is a significant
emphasis on sexual antagonism and sexuality here, to which
we shall return shortly. For in releasing the men's spirits by
consuming their bodies, the women are also considered to
be exacting vengeance on men for stealing the penis-like
initiation flutes that the women originally possessed.

This sexual complementarity is further elaborated in the
complex mortuary cannibalism of another New Guinea
people, the Bimin-Kuskusmin described by Fitzjohn Porter
Poole (1983). Here, male agnates honor the dead, counter-
acting the pollution of the mortuary rites by eating morsels of
the (male-substance) bone marrow of the deceased. This
ensures the passage of the dead man's spirit to the ancestral
underworld and the recycling of his procreative and ritual
strength within his patrilineage. Female agnates eat small
pieces of lower belly fat (female substance) to enhance their
reproductive and ritual powers. Although it is considered
particularly disgusting, penis flesh is even presented to the
widow, the eating of which is believed to enhance her fertility
and bind her productive power to the agnatic kin of the
deceased husband. Reciprocally, the ritually active husband of
a dead woman is expected to eat a fragment of her sexual
organ so as to enhance the fertility of her daughters. In all
these funeral contexts, the stress is on ensuring the fertility
and continuity of a group weakened by death. On the battle-
field, however, Bimin-Kuskusmin warriors add insult to
injury, expressing their contempt for defeated foes by eating
the feminine portions of their corpses and thus preventing
them from achieving full ancestor status (Porter Poole 1983:
15).

This brings us to the classical political context of cannibalism in the agonistic relations between hostile groups, the prime sacrificial victims being war captives or slaves (often similarly recruited). In this vein, Maori cannibalism – well-documented from contemporary nineteenth-century eyewitness accounts – was set in a context of ritual warfare; the consumption of human flesh paralleled that of birds and fish in hunting rituals. Men consumed at cannibalistic feasts were referred to as "fishes," and "first fish" being eaten by a chief who thus acquired control over the land of the vanquished. Victorious Maori chiefs are reported to have increased their *mana* by swallowing the eyes of their enemies.[9] In Fiji during the same period, chiefs of reputedly immigrant origin received tribute in the form of what Sahlins (1983: 80) calls "raw" women and supplied "cooked" men in communion feasts as largesse in return. The resources for this system of noblesse oblige were typically war captives or "internal" aliens in the form of rebels and dissidents. These sacrificial victims, "food for the gods," assumed divine status and were accorded the same terms of ritual reference as the body of a chief.

The ideas and symbols in play here achieve their most elaborate realization in Amazonian Indian ritual cannibalism. The Tupinamba of Brazil have long provided the locus classicus, known to Western scholars from the extensive, carefully documented sixteenth-century eyewitness accounts of the Portuguese Jesuit missionaries. Although Arens has attempted to discredit this picture of Tupi cannibalism by questioning the evidence in some of the more sensational popular accounts, the cumulative testimony is overwhelming and very convincing,[10] as Donald Forsyth (1983) has recently demonstrated in an impressively rendered reappraisal of the firsthand Jesuit evidence. The picture that emerges in these accounts is that the Tupi practiced ritual cannibalism extensively in the context of war and vengeance raids. Among the Tupinamba, who in common with so many other people married their enemies, a war captive was called a "loved one." Such prisoners, potential affines like the Tupi gods, were feted, provided with unmarried women as companions, and enjoyed luxury prisoner status for extended periods before they were ritually executed and consumed in an often orgiastic communion feast. Thus at the heart of the most sumptuous ritual cannibalism we encounter the theme of sexuality, which is also present in witchcraft. This is no coincidence. I do not think that we can reach any general understanding of the meaning and pervasive appeal of the ideology of cannibalism, and its use in labeling others and in interpreting their activities, unless we take due note of these sexual allusions.

As is well-known, eating and sexuality are closely related modes of intimate social interaction that readily flow together, both literally and metaphorically. In many, perhaps most, languages, including to some extent English, the same or similar expressions are used to refer to eating and making love. Consumed with desire, the lover eagerly seeks to devour the object of his passion. Terms of endearment, likewise, regularly compare the love object to a tempting dainty dish. In the contemporary Western world this equivalence or concurrence of the two modes of commensality – eating and sex – is appropriately reflected in the striking similarity in style and format between gourmet sex manuals and cookbooks. Some sex manuals, indeed, literally set out the stages of amorous play in the form of a menu; and sexual and culinary recipes lie side by side in the pages of journals like *Penthouse* and *Playboy*. Common expressions relating to love and sexual intercourse, such as "conquest" and "match," bear an obvious aggressive charge that is also present in the competitive elements of feasting and hospitality. In some African contexts, political usurpation is said to be represented as a process of seduction with the aid of tempting food.[11] In Fiji, according to Sahlins (1983: 79), a lowly commoner would grovel before a chief with the obeisance, "Eat me." Elsewhere "Be my guest!" is apt to be a challenge as well as an invitation. It is consequently scarcely necessary to refer to love bites, or *vagina dentata*, or indeed to the intermittent Western vogue for oral sex, to evoke the image of Dracula, the pan-human vampire, who so vividly embraces all these themes.

Ernest Jones[12] certainly recognized these parallels when he identified what he termed "oral sadism" in the concept of the vampire. For him this was a "regressive complex," provoked by the repression of normal adult genital sexuality. A typical if tragic illustration at the individual level would presumably be the case of the "cannibal of the Bois de Boulogne," the Japanese student in Paris who confessed to shooting and then eating an attractive Dutch girl who had rebuffed his advances and refused to sleep with him.[13] This is the sort of "abnormal" case that the psychoanalytic anthropologist Georges Devereux (1956) would no doubt characterize as "egodystonic." But a diagnosis of cannibalism, where it is a culturally accepted practice, as "culture dystonic" and hence indicative of general cultural malaise, is unlikely to appeal to the cultural-relativist anthropologist (cf. Geertz 1984). Similarly, Ernest Jones's rigid Freudian schema of evolutionary stages of sexual aggression seems today an excessive piece of psychoanalytic dogma. We surely no longer need to invoke the ideas of "regression" and "repression" to acknowledge a more flexible framework in which the different modes of sexuality inter-penetrate and flow into each other. From this perspective, linked as they are to oral and genital sexual aggression, the ideas of consumption, ingestion (see Porter Poole 1983), engulfment, and mastery clearly constitute potent symbols of power. Rooted in the universal human experiences of suckling, engaging in sex, and eating, these motifs provide the most pervasive thematic and emotional matrix for everything that pertains to the general phenomenon of cannibalism. It is therefore hardly surprising that, even when the practice of cannibalism has disappeared or has never existed, the *idea* of man-eating should survive as a latent force always capable, so long as beliefs in mystical power are sustained, of being evoked in myth and popular fantasy. The problem is not, as Arens (1979: 139) claims, that of explaining why people attribute cannibalism to their neighbors and enemies, but rather of understanding those cultures in which cannibalism is (or was) actually practiced as an integral part of ritual life. Here, as usual in the analysis of cultural forms, we may discern general thematic patterns associated with symbolic meanings recurring in similar ritual contexts. To attribute these, or other aspects of institutionalized culture, to such simple materialist "causes" as protein deficiency (Marvin Harris 1977), is in my opinion patently absurd.

CHAPTER 6

The shaman's career

I

The term *shaman* belongs to that special category of ethno-graphically specific concepts used cross-culturally outside their own native contexts. Other such "emic" terms are, of course, *caste*, *compadrazgo*, *mana*, *potlatch*, *tabu*, and perhaps *totem* and *voodoo*. These constitute a small but interesting category of originally culturally specific terms whose use, outside their native context, regularly engenders controversy and debate.

Although as Vilmos Voigt (1977: 385) justly observes in his admirable bibliographical critique, the "word shaman and the word Shamanism spread all over the world from Siberia," the currency of these terms varies considerably among the different national (and international) anthropological traditions and partly reflects regional ethnographic special-ization. They are well represented in the Scandinavian,[1] East European,[2] and continental traditions,[3] although perhaps less frequently in France.[4] In Italy, S. M. Shirokogoroff's classic account of Tungus shamanism, discussed later in this chapter, encouraged the influential historian of religion and man of letters Ernesto de Martino to launch a vigorous – and in his milieu at the time (1942) bold – attack on European ethno-centrism that ran contrary to the neo-Hegelian tradition of his own spiritual mentor, Benedetto Croce.[5]

In Anglophone anthropology, as so often elsewhere, there is a marked contrast here between American and British usage. With its Arctic (Eskimo) connections[6] and traditional Amerindian bias (more recently reinforced by South

American studies), and with the blessing of such founding fathers as Franz Boas,[7] the term "shaman" enjoys a secure position in American cultural anthropology. This is not the case in Britain, where the dominant structural-functionalist school has emphasized the contrasting concept *spirit-possession*, leaving shamanism to be subsumed under (or discarded as superfluous in distinction to) *spirit mediumship*. So, for instance, Godfrey Lienhardt's sensitive account of religious enthusiasm among the Dinka of the southern Sudan, *Divinity and Experience* (1961), contains more than twenty indexed references to possession – but not one to shamans or shamanism. If this had been the work of an American anthropologist, I suspect the terminology would have been rather different. Under such different ethnic sponsorship, Dinka shamans would surely by now have achieved a secure place in the ethnographic record.

The well-known British anthropologist S. F. Nadel's (1946) application of the term "shamanism" to the religious beliefs and practices of the peoples of the Nuba Hills of the Sudan is thus the exception that proves the rule (although it could perhaps be argued that Nadel had a more "continental" intellectual background than most of his contemporary British colleagues). The orthodoxy was, and remains, quite clear. Among mainline British social anthropologists and those American and other anthropologists strongly influenced by them,[8] concern continues over the propriety of the term "shaman," and it is consequently treated with grave reserve and used with marked reluctance. Following such earlier ventures as J. Beattie and J. Middleton's *Spirit Mediumship and Society in Africa* (1969), two recent symposia,[9] published in English but including contributions by French as well as American authors, similarly eschew the term "shamanism" in their titles – although the topic does materialize in their texts.

This hesitancy to accept the terms "shaman" and "shaman-ism" into standard British anthropological currency seems consistent with our emphasis on comparative analysis, our focus on societies rather than cultures, and our preference for "etic" rather than *"emic"* categories. We like to think that by employing external analytical terms having no cultural undercurrent except in our own English tradition we achieve greater precision and clarity and so avoid cultural confusion. Actually, however, as is becoming increasingly clear, such analytical categories become charged with an implicit cultural loading of their own derived from the exotic ethnographies to which we apply them. Even when we do not directly apply local folk categories outside their cultural contexts, we find that ethnographic regions still leave their imprint on our analytical vocabulary and color our theorizing. The pervasive, if not always persuasive, influence of Evans-Pritchard's use of Zande views of witchcraft and sorcery, or of Nuer lineages, has already been cited in this regard (Chapter 1).

With the transient exception of Nadel, the one major British anthropologist who has employed the term "shaman" is Raymond Firth – mainly to indicate a distant point on the horizon. Thus Firth (1967: 296) scrupulously distinguishes between "spirit-possession," "spirit mediumship," and "shamanism." Spirit-possession, Firth says, involves "phenomena of abnormal behaviour which are interpreted by other members of society as evidence that a spirit is controlling the person's actions and probably inhabiting his body." In "spirit mediumship" the accent, as Firth puts it, is on communication. Finally, "shamanism," Firth states, "applies to those phenomena where a person, either a spirit medium or not, is regarded as controlling spirits, exercising his mastery over them in socially recognised ways."

II

These distinctions seem at least to some extent to reflect the widespread influence of Mircea Eliade's magisterial work, *Le chamanisme et les techniques archaiques de l'extase* (1951). Eliade here purports to take us back to the Siberian Tungus ethnography, to which the word shaman is usually traced etymologically.[10] The shaman in this context is an inspired priest who in ecstatic trance states ascends, in spirit or soul, to the heavens on mystical "trips." He there meets and communes with the celestial powers in order to advance the interests of his fellow men. Spirit-possession is not directly connected with this. For Eliade "the specific element of shamanism is not the incorporation of spirits by the shamans but the ecstasy provoked by the ascension to the sky or by the descent to hell: the incorporation of spirits and possession by them are universally distributed phenomena, but they do not belong necessarily to shamanism in the strict sense." Indeed, the two elements can be separated historically: "The celestial ascent of the shaman is a survival, profoundly modified and sometimes degenerated, of the archaic religious ideology – centred on faith in a Celestial Supreme Being . . . the descent to Hell, the fight against evil spirits, and . . . the increasingly familiar relations with spirits which aim at their incorporation or at the possession of the shaman by them, are all *innovations*."[11]

Thus, according to Eliade, we may discern two historically distinct strata or evolutionary stages: first the authentic *shamanistic celestial ascent*, and second the subsidiary and diluting *possession by spirits*. In company with many other writers on the subject,[12] Eliade tends to associate the former "pure shamanism" (sometimes called "white shamanism" in the literature) with prehistoric Siberian hunter-gatherers and so with paleolithic cave art. Pater Schmidt[13] held precisely the opposite view, contending that primitive "black" shamanism was associated with matriarchy and an agrarian mode of production, and that the superior "white" shamanism, with its stress on celestial flight, developed only at a later stage associated with nomadism and patriarchy. Echoes of these evolutionary arguments recur in the writing of Soviet specialists who, as V. N. Basilov has observed, were bound to adopt a historical approach.

We shall return to these issues. For the moment our interest is in examining the ways in which Eliade's antithesis between celestial shamanic flight and spirit-possession has been elaborated and developed outside a historicist framework. Thus, disregarding its evolutionary overtones, the Belgian structuralist anthropologist Luc de Heusch (1962) has sought to make this dichotomy between celestial ascent and

Table 2. *de Heusch's "geometry of the soul"*

Adorcism	*Exorcism*
Insertion of soul spirit	Extraction of soul spirit
Shamanism A	*Shamanism B*
Shaman restores soul to patient, i.e., cures "soul-loss."	Shaman extracts foreign pathogenic spirit.
Possession A: "authentic"	*Possession B: "inauthentic"*
Injection of a new soul spirit	Extraction of foreign spirit

possession the springboard for an ingenious theory of contrasting religious phenomena. Here shamanism is seen as an "ascensual metaphysic" (a de-possession) and opposed to possession, which is seen as an incarnation. In line with Eliade, de Heusch regards these as characteristic of different cosmologies and religions. He distinguishes between *involuntary possession* by evil spirits, which are *exorcised*; and *voluntary possession* by good spirits, which are *incorporated*. The first he calls "inauthentic" possession, the second "authentic." The same distinctions are applied to shamanism and a fourfold structural matrix proposed (Table 2).

Acknowledging criticism of the overrigidity of this schema, de Heusch (1971) has since sought to trace transformations among these various categories of religious phenomena; in fact, he has come to see them as phenomenologically distinct types of trance. The authentic shamanistic trance, in its Amerindian or Siberian forms, de Heusch (1971: 270) asserts, "takes its position entirely in relation to therapy: the doctor is the general healer licensed in the course of – and by – trance . . . The trance state is, for a true shaman, that in which he operates *in a hot state*, with hyper-lucid agitation." The authentic shaman for de Heusch is essentially "clairvoyant" and endowed with the "extraordinary facility of seeing the spirits, of discovering them, of knowing their secrets and with the power of exorcising them.' The French ethnomusicologist Gilbert Rouget (1980) also accepts these distinctions, insisting (implausibly) that while all sorts of intermediate forms exist

between shamanism and possession, the distinction nevertheless remains "fundamental."

In a series of collaborative studies culminating in a
publication directed at a wide general readership, Erika
Bourguignon (1976) has pursued a similar path, seeking
correlations among different types of ecstatic states and
different societies or social formations. Her point of departure
is de Heusch's distinction between authentic and inauthentic
possession, which she labels "positive" and "negative"
respectively. Recognizing correctly that trance and possession
are not necessarily identical, Bourguignon sees "possession"
without trance (P) and possession with trance (PT) as opposed
religious phenomena associated with different modes of social
organization. The protean resources of G. P. Murdock's
Ethnographic Atlas are employed to explore how societies where
possession (P) occurs differ from those where possession-and-
trance (PT) hold sway. The author finds statistical justification for the conclusion that "P societies are on the whole less
complex than PT societies." "P societies," moreover, tend to
engage in hunting, gathering, and fishing, whereas "PT
societies" depend more heavily on agriculture and animal
husbandry for subsistence. This contrast Bourguignon
associates with child-rearing practices that encourage "self-
reliance, independence, initiative and achievement motivation" in hunting and gathering (P) societies, but *not* in
pastoral or agricultural (PT) societies. Since Bourguignon
(1976: 44–9) apparently associates possession (rather than
possession-trance) with shamanism, Eliade's ancient
shamanic hunters seem here to be hovering in the background.

Although she is more systematic (if in a rather mechanical
way) in her handling of comparative data, Bourguignon thus
falls into the same trap as de Heusch, where she is joined
inadvertently by Mary Douglas (1970). Douglas's attempts to
handle the problems posed by shamanism and possession
display the same basic fault – unjustified reification of cultural
categories and religions and emotional phenomena. Douglas
confidently assumes that whole societies (i.e. ethnic groups)

can be graded in terms of degrees of positive or negative emotional attitudes toward possession. Thus in the case of the Nilotic-speaking peoples of the southern Sudan, she asserts (on the basis of Evans-Pritchard 1956), that the Nuer fear trance and regard it as dangerous. The neighboring Mandari (Buxton 1973) are even more terrified of spirit-possession. By contrast the Dinka, Douglas claims, welcome trance with open arms, valuing it as a positive, beneficent experience. These gradations in culturally stereotyped attitudes (reified by Douglas) are claimed to correlate with corresponding gradations in "group and grid," vague concepts that Douglas employs to describe the "hold" different societies exert on individual members.

In this "test case," Douglas considers the social organization of the Mandari to be much more tightly integrated, with stronger constraints on its individual members, than that of the Dinka, which is loosely structured. In her schema, the Nuer lie midway between these extremes. As she puts it, somewhat elliptically: "For the Mandari, group is strongest; for the Nuer group is weaker but grid is strongest; for the Dinka, grid and group are weaker than for the Nuer" (Douglas 1970: 96). As anyone familiar with the ethnographic evidence will appreciate, this impressionistic assessment of variations in the political organization of these three Nilotic peoples is highly questionable. In terms of formality of political organization and group cohesion, it would be more convincing to locate the Dinka as lying between the Nuer (the epitome of uncentralized egalitarianism) and the Mandari, who are after all organized in small chiefdoms.

We must not be sidetracked, however, into a discussion of what for Mary Douglas is merely illustrative ethnography. The basic idea here is that loosely structured conditions encourage trance and possession, whereas tightly integrated structures discourage these abandoned styles of religiosity. "The weaker the social constraints, the more bodily dissociation is approved and treated as a central ritual adjunct for channeling benign power to the community. The stronger the social pressures, the more magicality in ritual and in the definition of sin"

(Douglas 1970: 97). More generally, according to the Durkheimian principle of "symbolic replication," religious feeling corresponds directly to the social conditions which, it is assumed, inspire it. We may note here that in line with the American culture and personality school of Whiting, Child, and others explicitly invoked by Bourguignon, Douglas implicitly assumes that undifferentiated emotional attitudes can be assigned to entire *societies* as though they were *individuals* with specific and predictable personalities. (It is thus unsurprising that Douglas should find direct parallels between the personalities of individuals and the "cosmologies" of societies.)

III

If it is in fact dubious whether stable attitudes toward emotive phenomena can be attributed even to individual personalities, it is certainly erroneous to imagine that in any meaningful sense whole cultures (so-called "societies") can be characterized as exhibiting "positive" or "negative" responses to trance and possession. Indeed, all the features that have been distinguished as signifying separate phenomena associated with contrasting social formations (past or present) actually regularly occur together within a single cultural context. This can be shown in various cultural settings; I shall take that of the Tungus as the model here. Anyone who takes the trouble to read carefully Shirokogoroff's masterpiece on Tungus shamanism, *The Psychomental Complex of the Tungus* (1935), will discover how superficial and simplistic are these other treatments of shamanism and possession. Like Bourguignon, the Tungus distinguish between possession (P) and possession-trance (PT), and also trance (T) without possession. So in Bourguignon's terms they are P, PT, and T all at once. Like de Heusch, they distinguish between desired and undesired possession by benign and evil forces. Thus these distinctions in attitudes towards trance and possession, which Douglas asserts to be typical of three different Nilotic societies, can all be found in the single cultural setting of the Tungus.

All these features, which others have seen as separate self-sustaining styles of religiosity, are in reality constituent elements in the composite shamanistic complex. Within this context (for they are not limited to it), the contrast that Bourguignon and de Heusch draw between negative and positive possession experiences corresponds regularly (although not exclusively) to serial phases in the assumption of the shamanistic career. Above all, *pace* de Heusch and Eliade, possession is not necessarily excluded by, or opposed to, shamanism. Let us return to Shirokogoroff (1935: 269), who tells us: "In all the Tungus languages the term (shaman) refers to persons of both sexes who have mastered spirits, who at their will can introduce these spirits into themselves and use their power over their spirits in their own interests, particularly helping other people who suffer from the spirits; in such a capacity they may possess a complex of special methods for dealing with the spirits." Often the shaman permanently incarnates these spirits (which may be those of his clan), which may manifest themselves when he is in a trance at a public seance – "shamanizing," as Shirokogoroff puts it. The shaman's body is a temple or tabernacle for the spirits, a vehicle or receptacle, what Shirokogoroff a little quaintly calls a "placing" and specifically differentiates from an icon.

This therapeutic vocation is typically announced by, and assumed, after a traumatic experience associated with hysteroid behavior interpreted as uncontrolled possession. "The shaman may begin his life career with a psychosis but cannot carry on his functions if he cannot master himself" (Shirokogoroff 1935: 366). The Tungus, Shirokogoroff stresses, distinguish between a person possessed by spirits and spirits possessed by the shaman. No one, he adds, is considered a shaman unless he can control spirits and introduce or expel them at will. At the beginning of his career he is supposed to have at least one spirit with whose help he can master other spirits. "No one can be accepted as a shaman unless he can demonstrably experience ecstasy – a half-delirious hysterical condition – 'abnormal' in European terms" (Shirokogoroff

1935: 274). This ecstatic state is achieved with the aid of a number of techniques: focusing the mind by staring fixedly into a brass mirror (which is regarded as a spirit "placing"); drumming and singing; inhaling of resinous smoke; drinking "a big cup of vodka"; smoking pipes of tobacco.[14] The spirits involved in this shamanistic seance, and more generally in the Tungus cosmology, cannot be simply classified as "good" or "bad" because (unlike Douglas, Bourguignon, and other ethnocentric anthropologists) the Tungus do not distinguish spirits in this unambiguous fashion. Any spirit, Shirokogoroff insists (1935: 121–2) may be malevolent, benevolent, or neutral, according to context and treatment, and more particularly depending on whether or not it is "mastered" by a shaman in relation to his local community.

Despite Eliade's emphasis on the theme of mystical flight to the "upper world," the Tungus, according to Shirokogoroff, actually place more stress on the shaman's spiritual voyages to the "lower world." More generally, he records that among all Tungus groups there are many occasions of shamanizing that are not concerned with either of these realms, but on the contrary with mastering spirits *in this world*. Examples cited include the liberation of a person from the spirits of a hostile shaman, or clan, or foreign spirits; the liberation of a clan from spirit attack; the expulsion of malevolent spirits and their mastering; sacrifice to benevolent or malevolent spirits; and divination of the causes of affliction with the aid of the shaman's auxiliary spirits. The essence of the shaman's role, Shirokogoroff insists, lies in his ability to incorporate potentially dangerous spirits into his own body, thus neutralizing or "mastering" them. This power to control spirits may, of course, be lost with age or in the competition with rival shamans; such judgments clearly reside with public opinion among the various Tungus clans. Although he notes exceptions, Shirokogoroff maintains that this ecstatic shaman who incarnates spirits typically differs from the elected clan priest, who is also designated by the word "shaman." Finally, we should note that at this time female shamans were almost as common as male shamans. This Shirokogoroff relates to what he considers an unusual degree of equality between the sexes among the Tungus. The general validity of Shirokogoroff's classical interpretation has been fully confirmed in the meticulous reexamination and masterly analysis of all the relevant Siberian ethnographic data by Anna-Leena Siikala, to whose illuminating model of the shaman's role we shall return.[15]

Further afield, Carmen Blacker's study[16] of Japanese shamanism provides confirmation of this composite picture of what one might call "Ur-shamanism," including uncontrolled primary and controlled secondary phases of possession behavior, the coexistence of trance and possession – sometimes combined, sometimes separate – and the presence of out-of-body shamanistic experiences (mystical flight) and spirit-possession. In the syncretic (Shinto-Buddhistic) Japanese religious tradition, Blacker stresses the complementary roles of two religious figures. These are the spirit-inspired medium (*miko*), a vessel through whom spirits speak to mortals, and the ascetic shaman proper (*shamon*). The latter is primarily a healer whose soul ascends to the heavenly cosmos, or who makes this journey here on earth through what Blacker calls "symbolic mimesis" – climbing mountains that represent spiritual ascent. Like his Tungus counterpart, the Japanese shaman has helping spirits and can indeed also incarnate spirits as well as sending his soul out on astral voyages. As Blacker (1975: 27) says, "Complementary though they may at first appear, the medium and the ascetic are closely bound together. Both must undergo the same ascetic practice before their particular kind of power can be acquired"; and "sometimes both kinds of power seem to be present, or at any rate overlapping, in the same person." In feudal Japan, "it was common to find . . . an ascetic husband married to a female medium."

Finally, to emphasize again how we may expect spirit-possession and shamanism, and possession and trance, to occur together in a single cultural setting, I cite Wazir-Jahan Karim's subtle analysis (1981) of shamanism among the Ma'Betisek aborigines of Malaysia. This careful study shows how the local term for shaman literally means a "person who becomes spirit-possessed." In the diagnostic healing seance, the shaman is possessed voluntarily by his "helping spirits" (introduced by the lordly Malay tiger spirits) and may or may not enter into a trance state. "The mental state of the performer whether in trance or not is not given much relevance; the state of spirit-possession is culturally explained by the audience according to set symptoms which appear in the seance. Trance-like states . . . are not an essential characteristic of a shamanistic seance" (Wazir-Jahan Karim 1981: 160). More generally, in certain contexts where it is unpredictable and uncontrolled, spirit-possession (associated with illness and madness) is avoided and feared, whereas in the shamanistic seance it is guided and controlled by the shaman.

IV

With these provisos and qualifications we can now characterize the shaman as an inspired prophet and healer, a charismatic religious figure with the power to control the spirits, usually by incarnating them. If spirits speak through him, he is also likely to have the capacity to engage in mystical flight and other "out of body experiences."[17] As Shirokogoroff amply documented for the Tungus, fully appreciating the implications, an initial traumatic experience or illness interpreted as possession is typically the passport which, through progressive involvement with spirits, leads to the assumption of the role that Raymond Firth and others have identified as that of the medium, and which in its turn may lead to the more active and managerial role of shaman – master (or mistress) of spirits. Indeed, as Mircea Eliade himself rightly argues[18] – and demonstrates with an impressive wealth of ethnographic evidence – from the point of view of the shaman this is in fact the standard pattern of "shamanistic initiation."

De Heusch, Bourguignon, and Douglas, it will be recalled, assumed with some variations that the phenomenological (subjective) quality of a "mystical" experience unambiguously

Table 3. *Interpretations of mystical experience*

Experience	Interpretation	Response
Bad, feared, "inauthentic," "negative"	Devil	Exorcism (cf. shock treatment)
Good, appreciated, "authentic," "positive"	God	Domestication (cf. psychoanalysis)

determined its evaluation in terms of the mystical force (or forces) to which it would be attributed and the corresponding ritual action or treatment (Table 3).

In reality, however, the initial experience is usually in essence ambiguous or ambivalent and admits of two contrasting possible responses – exorcism (rejection), or domestication (acceptance, introjection, identification). In the latter case, the spirit or spirits responsible for the initial (and retrospectively initiatory) trauma are subsequently transformed into "helping spirits" by a process recalling that referred to by psychologists as "identifying with the aggressor." As I have already argued, these mystical encounters are *not* characteristic of different cultures, evolutionary stages, modes of production, and so forth, but regularly (although not invariably) coexist in a single cultural setting and period. Indeed, as Anna-Leena Siikala[19] shrewdly observes, such ostensibly diametrically opposed phenomena as pathogenic demonic possession and spirit-inspired shamanizing are, in practice, likely to be mutually reinforcing.

If we now expand the domestication (rather than exorcism) response, we can readily discern what is, I believe, the fundamental structure of shamanistic initiation. Here the initial traumatic experience signaling spiritual attention becomes a divine call, all the more impressive because its unsolicited, traumatic character establishes the bona fides of the new recruit as one forced by the overwhelming power of the spirits into their service. As the new devotee protests his or her unworthiness, so he or she establishes all the more securely the inevitability and authenticity of the "call." (Such striking

Table 4. *Episodic model of the ecstatic/shamanistic career*

Phase I	Phase II	Phase III
"Involuntary, uncontrolled, unsolicited" possession (or other seizure, e.g., illness or other trauma) ——————→	Accommodated, domesticated ————→	Controlled, voluntary, solicited trance
Patient ———————————————————————→		Healer

declarations of shamanistic election repay close scrutiny.) Hence the shamanistic career is a true "cult of affliction," to use the term favored by V. Turner (1969), A. L. Siikala,[20] and myself (Lewis 1971: 66ff.).

This initiatory process (Table 4) includes at least three quite well-defined Van Gennepian phases, episodes, or perhaps better "roles." For clarity of description and analysis we should distinguish such states or roles as carefully as possible. Trance and possession should not be confused, unless they coincide. At the same time we should recognize the limits of such classification and the confusion and distortion that excessive reification promotes. A rigid adherence to the term "spirit medium" because it seems safe, when shaman would be more appropriate, often serves to conceal rather than reveal significant common sociological features. In fact many – perhaps most – of those described in the ethnographic literature as "spirit mediums" (e.g., the Malaysian *bomoh* or modern Western spirit medium) have spirit familiars at their command. It is with the aid of these "spirit guides" that in seance contexts they diagnose and resolve the problems of their clients. They are thus "masters of spirits" and so shamans.[21] It must of course be understood, as Shirokogoroff demonstrates, that shamans can also *lose* their mastery over spirits and risk relapsing, in terms of our model, into the role of patient.

This regression is linked to the judgment that powers once

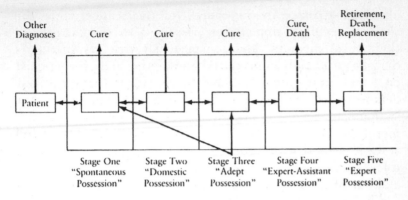

Figure 1 Paradigm of the individual possession career

controlled for the protection and benefit of the community are now unleashed to threaten the well-being of the group. Mastery of the spirits remains ultimately provisional, and the shaman whose powers are judged to be waning, perhaps in competition with new aspirants, readily becomes a target for witchcraft accusations – which as we have seen may include charges of cannibalism. Our episodic processural model thus serves to clarify the assumption, abuse, and loss of shamanic authority; it also emphasizes the volatility, permeability, and reversability of these roles. This is why individually the terms *possessed person*, *spirit medium*, and *shaman* are not very helpful typologically at the cultic or cultural level. Indeed, our tripartite model stressing how these states overlap and flow together is probably too condensed and abbreviated; it should be expanded into a full paradigm of the "possession career," as indicated in Figures 1 and 2 (after Alice Morton, 1973). This five-stage schema traces the sequence of possession contexts from the initial, spontaneously possessed patient stage to that of professional expert-healer. Potential drop-out from further possession cult involvement is available at each stage through "cures" that remove the individual from the cycle of spirit-possession.

To the extent that they frequently recapitulate the shaman's own initiatory experiences, these various roles may also be actualized in the context of the seance. Here the shaman regularly appears as possessed by spirits, acts as their vocal medium, and conspicuously masters them. As Shirokogoroff fully appreciated and as the French surrealist poet and ethnographer Michel Leiris (1958) has sensitively demonstrated for Ethiopian possession and shamanism, the shamanistic seance is high theater.[22] The shaman does not merely act or perform, but rather assumes and enacts with full ecstatic virtuosity what Anna-Leena Siikala calls his "counter-roles" – the materializations of his spirit guides. He moves in and out of a series of trance states of varying intensity, but rarely loses contact with his audience (however oblivious he may seem).

If the seance provides the natural setting for the enactment of the shaman's richly stored repertoire of roles, shamanism itself seems best defined along the lines indicated by the Russian scholar V. N. Basilov[23] – "a cult whose central idea is the belief in the ability of some individuals chosen by some spirits to communicate with them while in a state of ecstasy and perform the functions of an intermediary between the world of spirits and the given human collective (collectivity)." Although there is much to be said for it, this view does not necessarily entail unreservedly endorsing the belief of Basilov and other Soviet specialists that shamanism is essentially a "pre-class" religion that may nevertheless survive in class societies in a marginal, peripheral cult form. It does not matter how the balance between possession and soul-flight is pitched, whether or not a three-tier cosmology is present (though often it is), nor whether Vivianne Paques's (1964) "cosmic tree" is part of the picture (though often it is). These and many other symbolic motifs are widely if not universally associated with shamanism. There are many local variations in cosmology that are not intrinsically linked to shamanism. As Shirokogoroff himself constantly emphasizes, Tungus religion and cosmology are not static phenomena – historically and geographically they have been influenced by culture borrowing and exchange on a wide front, with the shaman playing a crucial innovative role as receiving agent and

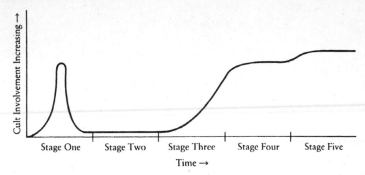

Figure 2 The possession career in relation to cult involvement

mediator for alien spiritual forces. There is abundant evidence of significant external influence from Chinese, Manchu, and Buriat, to say nothing of Russian, sources. Buddhism also seems to have played a powerful role in shaping Tungus religion, although by the second decade of this century the majority of the population had become "nominal" Christians, according to Shirokogoroff. Syncretism remained the order of the day; the Russian St. Nicholas had been adopted by the Tungus as the "grand master" of shamans. There is a remarkable correspondence between this protean figure and our contemporary European and North American image of Santa Claus, flying through the skies with his reindeer-drawn sleigh, laden with miraculous gifts.

Such homely allusions will not, I trust, distract the reader from the central intention of this chapter, which by applying a processual, developmental model seeks to elucidate the concept "shaman," restoring it to its proper context in the possession career. This exercise in unpacking an ethnically specific term for what is actually the very epitome of charismatic authority may, it is hoped, contribute to a more informed understanding of universal religious roles, which for too long have been treated as though they represented different species beyond the reach of effective comparative analysis.

CHAPTER 7

Expelling spirits,
controlling women

I

As we have seen in previous chapters, there are essentially two
contrasting responses to conditions which are interpreted as
spirit-possession. Exorcistic procedures may be invoked to
drive out the spirit(s), or attempts may be made to placate the
spirits by cultivating a viable (and often enduring) relationship with them. This second process of spirit accommodation
or internalization (termed "adorcism" by de Heusch 1962;
1971) usually amounts to a form of initiation, recruiting adepts
through illness into a "cult of affliction" (Turner 1969). The
status of the resulting ecstatic cult, as either a central or
peripheral movement, depends, it seems (Chapter 3), largely
on the moral identity of the spirits involved and on the
social status of the majority of those who succumb to spirit
afflictions. So, in full-blown, male-dominated ecstatic
religions, men are possessed by those spirits which uphold
morality and the cosmos, whereas, as we have seen in earlier
chapters, women may be plagued by marginal spirits – often of
alien origin.

Such "peripheral" spirits, however, also frequently trouble
women (and some marginalized men) in religious traditions
where possession and ecstasy are, in contrast, *not* significant
features of the main, male-dominated cult. In such circumstances, exorcism, and adorcism obviously have very different
consequences. The first upholds and entrenches the power of
the exorcising agencies and those who administer them. The
second, in contrast, cultivates the power of the invasive,

peripheral spirits, with the formation of what are essentially women's cults which have a subversive potential. From the point of view of the male religious establishment, at best, women are here engaged in obscure therapeutic activities: at worst, they are involved in dangerously superstitious traffic with occult forces which threaten the established religious order. Exorcism, therefore, is likely to appeal to members of the dominant male religious establishment, whereas adorcism is more attractive to women. Men favor exorcism as a means of containing adorcism, and if they are successful, exclude it completely. Viewed in this light, exorcism represents aborted adorcism: spirit-possession is stopped in its tracks, reversed, and prevented from flowering into formalized adorcism. In selecting exorcism, men, I argue, seek not only to control female adorcism and so maintain their control of women, but also to emphasize the dominance of male establishment religiosity. On the other hand, female adorcism represents a reaction by women to oppressive male religiosity, usually in conditions of social change in which the position of women deteriorates (cf. Lewis 1989: 12).

To examine the interplay between these two contrasting styles of spirit "management" I turn to consider certain well-documented cases involving what are generally considered to be male-dominated "World Religions" – Christianity, Islam, and Buddhism. My examples make no pretence to be exhaustive, but they do, I believe, indicate general patterns. I begin with cases in which *both* exorcism and adorcism are present, and move to others where, apparently, only exorcism is available. Exorcism occurs in all my examples.

In our opening case (Christian Ethiopian *zar*), where we do not know the historical circumstances in which the spirit cult arose, our primary concern is to establish the contrasting implications of the two alternative treatments. Our second example (the West African Muslim *bori* cult) illustrates how the adoption of the male-dominated religion of Islam can, through the constrictions it imposes on women, generate a reactive spirit cult offering an attractive alternative to exorcism. Similarly in our third case, the expansion and intensification of male-biased Buddhism in Burma has prompted a parallel feminization of the "traditional" spirit cult, creating a situation in which both exorcism and adorcism are again available treatment options. In the related case of Buddhist Sri Lanka (our fourth example) we encounter a situation in which the spirit cult, produced by adorcism, has developed quite rapidly in response to a marked decline in the socio-economic circumstances of women and a rise of "fundamentalist" Buddhism among the political elite. This, more clearly perhaps than our other cases, indicates the essentially dynamic interplay between exorcism and adorcism and how increasing reliance on the former by the male religious establishment is, under appropriate conditions, likely to encourage the development of the latter as an alternative healing process. It shows also, however, how exorcism can exist on its own without necessarily provoking adorcism. This is further indicated by our final case in which we return to Islam, this time in the context of Malaysia. This Malay material in turn prompts us to reconsider the relationship between male power and exorcism.

II

The attractions of exorcism for husbands and of adorcism for wives as ritual responses to the spirit afflictions to which women are especially prone is highlighted in modern accounts of the famous *zar* cult among the dominant ethnic groups of Christian Ethiopia (Young 1975; Morton 1977). This ecumenical cult, which is elaborately developed also in the neighboring Islamic states of Somalia, the Sudan, and Egypt (cf. Lewis *et al.* 1991: 81–230), includes many Muslim and other non-Christian elements, and is strongly condemned by the (male) clerical establishment of the Ethiopian orthodox church. The *zar* spirits, which like much else in Ethiopia, are traced back to Adam and Eve, are regarded as being unequivocally evil by the church. Although men are not entirely exempt, *zar* spirits prey particularly upon women, causing a wide range of illnesses. Common symptoms of illness affecting women which are apt to be interpreted as spirit-caused afflictions include: malaise, listlessness, chronic stomach pains, headaches, fevers, etc. The presenting illness, and the *zar* spirit believed to be causing it, are both referred to by a term which also means to shackle a prisoner – indicating the power the spirit has over its victims.

In the wider Christian cosmology, *zar* spirits fall loosely within the general category of evil demons of which many other than *zars* exist that are capable of possessing people and causing illness. Since different pathogenic spirits may cause the same symptoms, different interpretations and treatments are available for the same syndrome. Diagnosis in terms of spirit etiology raises the possibility of three lines of traditional treatment. Before pursuing these, however, it should be noted that the same symptoms may also be interpreted as due to more mundane factors than spirits and treated pragmatically by herbalists. This is reported to be the least expensive remedy (Young 1975: 574). If herbal treatment fails, the patient is likely to consult one or more of the three types of specialist spirit healer. Two of these specialists – dealing with "demons" rather than *zar*, although the distinction is blurred (Leiris 1980: 12ff.) – draw upon the power of the Ethiopian Orthodox Church to *exorcise* pathogenic spirits. At a number of famous church shrines, priests have acquired renown, sometimes even nationally, as divinely inspired healers, using the baptism ritual to expel evil spirits from the bodies of the possessed.

Much more widely available throughout Ethiopia are the services of itinerant clerics (*dabtaras*) who employ astrological techniques of diagnosis and treat possessed victims by means of amulets, offerings, sacrifice, and exorcism. Although these treatments derive their efficacy ultimately from the divine power invested in the church, the *dabtaras* are also considered by the lay public to enjoy the support of spirit familiars. This, thus, links them with the third and least prestigious category of spirit healer – the shamanic leader (*bala-awlya*) of a *zar* cult group whose treatments are based on adorcism rather than exorcism (for details see Leiris, 1980).

Forbidden to non-Christians, the exorcism practised by male clerical healers mobilizes the awesome might of the church to expel demonic forces which are officially anathematized. The contrasting shamanic treatment by adorcism, placates and celebrates precisely such "heretical" spirits. Conducted mainly by female shamans, it typically obliges the patient to seek relief by joining the *zar* cult coterie, an organization which, with pagan and Muslim associations and close links with prostitution, is perceived as extremely threatening and degrading to respectable members of the Orthodox Church.

In Ethiopia, as elsewhere, however, the best treatments are apt to be the most expensive. Hence, despite its high initial cost, a status-conscious farmer in the central Ethiopian highlands is likely to prefer that his sick wife should be treated by Christian exorcism and will endeavor to steer her in this direction rather than surrender her to the attentions of a *zar* shaman. Whatever psycho-social component there may be in precipitating the wife's possession affliction, conflict between the couple is likely to arise or intensify in deciding which of these conflicting treatments to pursue. Constrained by the preferred male treatment, wives in economically viable Christian households are reported to be likely to experience occasional bouts of sickness attributed to the *zar* spirits, but with their treatment limited to occasional shamanic inter-action and stopping short of full initiation into the *zar* cult (Young 1975: 582). In such socio-economic circumstances the latter course would be likely to provoke or sanction the break-up of marriage, helping to maintain the cult's negative image, in the eyes of the Christian establishment, as a haven for abandoned wives, divorcees, and prostitutes – especially in towns.

Evidently here, exorcism, which costs more money (at least initially) preserves formal male control and dignity in the name of Christian orthodoxy, and the exorcists are, significantly, men. (As in other Christian denominations, the Orthodox Ethiopian Church admits women as nuns – but they do not practise as clerical exorcists and women are generally too "unclean" to attend formal church services.) On the other hand, the initially less expensive shamanic treatment appeals to women who, for one reason or another, seek help and fulfilment in the subversive *zar* cult which embraces a syncretic cosmology of Christian, Muslim, and "pagan" spirits – itself a replica of the real world of contemporary religious pluralism in Ethiopia. Here, as in other parts of the world, women may exact a high price for male pride.

III

I turn now to review briefly the similar interplay of exorcism and domestication (adorcism) in the treatment of pathogenic spirits in an Islamic context. This concerns the equally famous *bori* spirits as they manifest themselves among the Hausa-speaking peoples of West Africa. Like *zar*, with which, indeed, they blend and merge in the Sudan (see Lewis *et al.* 1991: 35–80), the *bori* spirits and their cult have spread widely into Muslim North Africa (Tremeárne 1914; Dermenghem 1954). However, our present concern here is limited to the West African Hausa context. Here, although Islam has for several centuries been the dominant faith of the Hausa and, as is well known, has found militant expression in many far-reaching holy wars, there still exist pockets of non-Muslim Hausa who adhere to the "traditional" pre-Islamic religion. In the dominant Muslim society, elements of these beliefs have been marginalized and feminized in the shape of the *bori* spirit possession cult, a true "cult of affliction" in which spirit-possessed women patients may become initiated devotees – "mares of the gods" (see Monfouga-Nicolas 1972; Echard 1978; Besmer 1983).

This subversive and primarily female cult, whose leaders are divorced women and prostitutes, is perceived as an affront to official male Muslim respectability, perhaps even more directly than the *zar* cult in Ethiopia because it is known to derive (however syncretically) from pre-Islamic times. The male religious establishment endeavours to control it in two, contradictory ways. On the one hand, men attempt to control wives with spirit-afflictions by engaging the services of Islamic exorcists – the multipurpose Muslim clerics known locally as *malams*. On the other hand, historically the male establishment of the hierarchical Hausa states co-opted the *bori*-cult, by assigning official court titles to cult leaders and incorporating them in the state structures. Thus, for orthodox Hausa men, diagnosis and treatment by female *bori* shamanic specialists represents a "therapy of last resort" for their wives (Nicolas 1975: 211; cf. Last 1976; 1979). It is not surprising that the relations between *malam* Muslim exorcist and *bori* cult leader are apt to be antagonistic, especially on the part of the former (Abdalla 1991).

For women, particularly the secluded wives of bourgeois husbands, the *bori* cult has a strong appeal as the circumstances of contemporary Islamic conversion among residual "pagan" groups indicate. In the wider West African setting here, a Muslim is referred to as one who "prays" in contrast to the non-Muslim who, as the Hausa say, "drinks beer." (In keeping with this and in competition with Nigerian advertisements for Coca Cola and Scotch whisky, Islam is advertised as "The wise man's choice.") When a non-Muslim decides to embrace Islam and give up alcohol, his wife, who fears curtailment of her traditional "pagan" freedom, is apt to join the alternative *bori* cult. For a man, the cost of conversion to Islam is considerable, for with the entailed domestic seclusion of his wife he loses most of her labor services as well as having to pay for her *bori* episodes. These costs, and those involved in joining a trading network (which is normally associated with conversion) are, apparently, not compensated for by the saving on beer-party expenditure (Last 1979). Recourse to Islamic exorcism to control, or ideally counter, the *bori* outbursts of a rebellious wife may entail further expense.

In this Islamic context, as with *zar* in Christian Ethiopia, men employ male exorcists representing the male-dominated establishment religion as the preferred treatment for the spirit afflictions of their women folk. This "masculine" therapy is in competition with the women's own remedies which, from a male point of view, may be initially less costly but are far more disruptive of male interests. The rival therapies reflect the conflicting interests of female patients and the men who are responsible for them. In this particular case, in addition to utilizing exorcism, the male religious establishment seems to have, as it were, hedged its bets by bestowing formal state titles on *bori* cult leaders, thus co-opting the movement within the traditional Hausa politico-ritual hierarchy. This, as I see it, additional male device of female containment seems also to be present in the next case I want to examine.

IV

Amongst the World Religions, the Muslim and Christian traditions have no monopoly of exorcism and adorcism. I turn now to consider the interplay of these alternative healing practices in the Buddhist contexts of Burma and Sri Lanka – first the Burmese *nat* spirit cult. Analogously to *bori*, the *nat* cult is a syncretic development of indigenous pre-Buddhist Burmese religion and persists in uneasy tension with the official state religion of Buddhism (Spiro 1967; 1978). These two "religions" (here I follow Spiro 1978: xxxff.) exist in parallel and interpenetrate at many points in such a way that the *nat* cult is legitimized by Buddhism and, at the same time, subordinated to it. So, the Buddhist "King of the Thirty-seven *nats*" presides over the *nat* hierarchy and is "pre-eminent" in the Buddhist New Year festival. Similarly, prominent *nat* spirit shrines are frequently located on mountains just below Buddhist pagodas. More generally, *nat* rituals which are principally directed by women are often followed by Buddhist rites performed by men. Despite this elaborate parallelism, the *nat* cult, according to Spiro, expresses opposition to Buddhism and has not lost its subversive character by being incorporated within the territorial and administrative structure of the historical Burmese Kingdom, and prominent *nat* spirits receive annual "tribute" at their provincial shrines in the same manner as the feudal provincial lord. In a direct sense, Spiro (1978: 132ff.) argues that this *nat* cult,

historically, was instituted by the Burmese kings to serve
political ends.

More recently, in a similar fashion to the *bori* cult, the *nat*
religion has been feminized and partially marginalized by
male-dominated Buddhism. The *nat* spirits – condemned
by men as evil and capricious in comparison with benevolent
Buddhist deities (*devas* – of Hindu origin) – are particularly
closely associated with women. Women's illnesses may be
diagnosed as "malevolent" possession by *nat* spirits. Our two
main types of treatment are again available: adorcism and
exorcism. The former involves engaging the services of a *nat*
inspired shaman. These healers, most of whom are women,
are typically ex-patients, recruited through initiatory episodes
which are interpreted as involving a love affair with a
nat-spirit. With full initiation this leads to a formal, and
expensive, *nat*-wedding, the shaman being referred to literally
as a "*nat*-wife," whose lusty spiritual sex life contrasts quite
sharply with the asexual asceticism of the contemplative
Buddhist monk. It is these intimate relations with *nat* spirits
which empower shamans to diagnose and treat – ultimately by
means of adorcism – *nat* afflictions in other women. What
empowers female healers here, as elsewhere, also contributes
to their condemnation, by men, as sexually immoral and
promiscuous creatures associated with evil spirits and vulgar
"superstition." The alternative treatment of exorcism is
conducted by male Buddhist specialists employing superior
Buddhist magic and the aid of benevolent Buddhist deities to
drive out the *nats*. These "masters of the Upper Path" as they
are called, belong to messianic Buddhist associations (see
Spiro 1978: 230ff. and Mendelson 1961) in which they practise
Buddhist devotions and engage in meditations. Although their
status is lower than that of Buddhist monks, they nevertheless
represent the cutting edge of the official male-dominated
religion in its was against *nat* demons. Thus, once again, male
power is buttressed by the exorcistic treatment option (in this
case, according to Spiro, not particularly expensive), and by
the co-option, under official patronage, of what has become a
subversive female cult.

In Buddhist Sri Lanka, on the other hand, modern accounts of spirit-afflictions, such as that of Kapferer (1983), stress exorcism as the typical treatment and make no reference to adorcism. The prevalence of largely working class and peasant female victims, here, is explained culturologically by Kapferer (1983: 92) – who evidently thinks that culture explains itself – as a "function" of the "cultural typification" which places women "in a special and significant relation to the demonic." Moreover, according to him, "demonic attack symbolises the subordination of a Sinhalese working class and peasantry who are caught in an obdurate world, weakened in its structure, and who are socially and politically fragmented . . . Demons are the terrors which prowl at the base of hierarchy . . . a hidden power waiting to break free."

These pathogenic spirits plaguing women are regarded as signs of disorder, and the exorcistic rituals employed to treat them seek to restore the ideal Buddhist cosmic order. Here, as we should by now expect, exorcism is performed by male agents of this Buddhist order – specifically members of the *berava* service "caste." Such exorcisms appear to underline and strengthen male-dominated Buddhist ideology and power as the nationalistic, revitalized Buddhist middle classes seek to distance themselves from practices which, in their discourse, represent low-class "primitive survivals" opposed to their construction of Buddhism.

This picture is, however, no longer complete. As Gombrich and Obeyesekere (1988) elegantly demonstrate with more convincing, sociological analysis, while such exorcism was the only "traditional" response in cases of women's spirit possession, in recent years the alternative treatment of adorcism has become very popular. Both treatments are thus now available, and however much men may prefer their possessed wives to be treated by exorcism, many women now succeed in pursuing the alternative of adorcism. Thus, today, the conversion of patients into priestesses is proliferating at urban shrines. "The (new) theory of divine possession enhances the self-respect of the possessed person and becomes a source of 'liberation' (increased dignity, social independence, earning power) for women and indeed many other people who see no hope of other success of fulfilment" (Gombrich and Obeyesekere 1988: 41). In conditions of severe overpopulation, with a steep rise in the age of marriage (especially for women), chronic unemployment and pauper- ization, and the breakdown of traditional extended kin ties, such spirit cult groups – in which women predominate – can be seen to provide fictional or substitute kin groups for the alienated urban proletariat (Gombrich and Obeyesekere 1988: 67ff.). In response to these socio-economic changes and the rise of conservative "Protestant Buddhism" women, and some marginalized men seek relief from affliction in the reactive, revitalized spirit cult (heavily influenced by Hinduism) which male-dominated Buddhism brands as demonic.

v

Finally, I return to Islamic exorcism, this time in the context of Malaysia where, no counterpoised female cult, based on adorcism, is reported in the literature. Here the most analytically impressive modern account of this "traditional" treatment, in Kelantan state, is provided by Kessler (1977: see also Firth 1967; Endicott 1970; Laderman 1987, 1991). The majority of patients with spirit-caused afflictions dealt with in this way were women who may be grouped in three categories: (1) young brides forced against their will to marry husbands of their parents' choosing; (2) middle-aged wives reacting to the problems of polygyny; (3) widows and divorcees. Various presenting symptoms (sometimes associated with organic illnesses ranging from malaria to tuberculosis; in other cases psychosomatic) are diagnosed and treated by specialist male exorcists called *bomohs*.

The classic treatment takes the form of a highly dramatic exorcistic seance in the course of which, with the aid of his own spirit familiar(s), the *bomoh* first identifies the pathogenic spirit involved, and then summons an appropriate healing spirit to possess him and drive out the malignant force. The successful expulsion of the pathogenic spirit is indicated when the patient dances in a trance state with the *bomoh* at the climax of the healing rite. Known literally as "princess play" (*main peteri* – and by other names in other Malay states) this exorcistic seance is strongly charged with royal (and political) symbolism. In the course of the ritual, the patient dances to tunes from shadow puppet plays, evoking the heroic battles of Ramayana, or courtly scenes from the *mak yong* folk operas. According to Kessler, explicit analogies are drawn between the patient's disordered physical state and a disordered body politic – a "disarticulated realm" to which regal authority, invoked here by the *bomoh*, restores order and well-being by exorcising the spirit responsible.

Although the role of *bomoh* seems to hark back to pre-Islamic times and incorporates many more recent non-Islamic influences, the male exorcist presents himself as a local agent of the cosmic hierarchy, presided over by Allah, sovereign of the universe. Thus, however aggressively female patients may appropriate male roles in the seance dramas, in the end the subversive spirits involved are triumphantly expelled and the male-dominated Islamic order is restored by the healing statecraft of the male exorcist. From the male point of view, whatever the material costs to the patient's kin, the spirit of female subversion is held in check by extracting and exorcising it from the patient's body which is a microcosm of the body-politic. It is not able to flower into a separate, gender-specific cult, based on adorcism. Or so it appears.

Since the literature seems generally silent on this point, I made it the focus of a brief and inevitably rather superficial survey I conducted in the summer of 1988 of the practises of rural *bomohs* in Penang Island.[1] This region is of particular interest because it is, effectively, the "silicone chip valley" of Malaysia with a high density of industrial concentration of multinational electronics and computer companies, drawing their labor force primarily from the female population of surrounding Malay villages. Trade union activity is not permitted, and labor problems are apt to find expression in the outbreaks of spirit possession amongst female employees for which this industrial zone is famous (Ackerman and Lee

1981; Ong 1987). Thus spirit possession, originating in this context as well as in others (including girls' schools) is a common complaint which *bomohs* are engaged to treat.

I interviewed eleven *bomohs* in the surrounding Malay villages and observed the practise over several days of a smaller number. The first point to note is that five of these were *women*, and although I cannot cite authoritative national statistics I gather that this high proportion of female village *bomohs* is not unusual in rural Malaysia (cf. Werner 1986). The villages concerned are all very accessible to the main roads (and factories) of Penang and all these *bomohs* lived in comfortable houses, well-equipped with such modern facilities as televisions and telephones, the latter being extensively used by clients to book appointments and also to seek the *bomohs'* advice. Their houses, where they receive their clients, are variously decorated with Islamic mottoes and signs, as are their spirit shrines which, however, usually also include a rich array of devices and images of Indonesian, Thai, and Hindu provenance – as well as sundry magic stones, swords, daggers, sticks, and pieces of wood from aboriginal Malay sources. All these are employed in magical treatments, using incense, betel leaves, limes and flowers, with spells and incantations (*jampis*) drawn from the Quran and manuals of magical formulae, obtained from the practitioner's gurus. They are additionally activated and empowered through the force of the *bomoh*'s helping spirits (*hantu*), which may include spirit spouses, ancestors, tiger spirits, and Muslim saints (*walis*). Without distinction, these are all said to act under the general and overriding direction of *Allah*. Some *bomohs* – a minority of those I interviewed – practice in trance. Others do not, and some are very skeptical of what they refer to as "so-called" trance activity. None of the Penang *bomohs* I met belonged to the National Association of Traditional Healers, an organization founded in 1979 to promote the professionalization of *bomohs* in the modern context and claiming successful treatment of drug addition and, more recently, AIDS.

Patients, male and female, but especially the latter, and

of all ethnic groups (Malay, Chinese, Indian, as well as European, Australian, and American tourists) consult these *bomohs* about a wide spectrum of complaints, ranging from illnesses like diabetes to psycho-sexual problems (very prominent), work-related issues (securing employment and promotion), and the recovery of missing persons (e.g. spouses) and possessions. Various kinds of psychic disturbance and states which are diagnosed as spirit possession (often ascribed to an enemy's spell), particularly in women, are also handled by *bomohs*.[2] Possession is treated by exorcism, by both male and female *bomohs* using similar techniques. Although a series of therapeutic sessions may be necessary in stubborn cases, the procedure I observed here (and was told about) is much less elaborate than the traditional Kelantan *main peteri* ritual which, indeed, a number of *bomohs* maintained was forbidden as being un-Islamic. Essentially the process is as follows. With the aid of his or her familiar spirits, and the all-encompassing authority of *Allah* (invoked with differing emphasis by different *bomohs*), the *bomoh* interrogates the patient's possessing spirit(s), asking why it (or they) have possessed the patient, and then ordering them to leave their victim who is fumigated with incense and bombarded with powerful incantations (*jampis*). This exorcistic treatment, in the cases I have observed or was told about, was supplemented with medicines such as charmed betel leaves, limes, and bathing with water from a mosque. Such possessing spirits may also be cajoled into releasing their victims by offerings of gifts and food. The fees charged are at the discretion of the patient's accompanying kin, and vary considerably between small token amounts and substantial cash payments.

So far as I could establish, the treatment here is properly categorized as "exorcism," since it is designed to expel the spirit rather than to accommodate it, or build up an ongoing relationship between it and its human victim. Thus, treatment here does not serve as initiation into a cult based on adorcism, and does not launch the patient into a possession career, culminating in the role of *bomoh*.

While in a few cases, men or women become *bomohs* after

successfully overcoming illness, this is not necessarily in a possession context, and is by no means the general pattern. Typical recruitment processes, indicated in my small survey, are through inheritance from an ancestor; through inspirational dreams; as a consequence of miraculous cures unexpectedly effected on members of one's family or neighbors; and, usually later in a *bomoh*'s career, by studying under famous gurus in various parts of Malaysia, Thailand, and Indonesia. Thus, I conclude from this brief survey, that while clients, especially those with matrimonial and related problems, frequently consult favorite *bomohs* quite regularly, there is no evidence here of *bomoh*-led cult groups, and no female cults of affliction based on adorcism. Like their male colleagues, women *bomohs* practise exorcism *not* adorcism.

VI

Although constitutionally, exorcism and adorcism appear to be dialectically opposed processes, exorcism, as we have seen, can indeed exist on its own, preventing rather than provoking the counter reaction of adorcism. Or, to put it differently, adorcism may not succeed in being installed as a formal alternative to exorcism.

However, the situation seems to be more complex than our simple dichotomy suggests. In particular, we need to subject the process of exorcism itself to closer scrutiny. As the case of Malay Islam indicates, the exorcists who uphold a male-dominated religion by exorcising unruly spirits which trouble women, may include women. This might, of course, be seen as an instance of women colluding in their own oppression. But in the Malay context this seems a doubtful interpretation since the reality is rather that mainstream Malay Islam views *bomohs* of either sex as dubious practitioners, involved with powers which the most orthodox are prone to condemn as heretical. This, no doubt, is one reason why – whatever their actual historical origins – in contemporary Malaysia *bomohs* are understandably anxious to stress the Islamic foundations of their practice. From a less culturally subjective standpoint, the fact that women can work as *bomohs* accords women a major role in the practise of *popular* Malay Islam, tempering male dominance of the official cult. Hence, perhaps, the absence of adorcism.

Of course, all this could change radically. In the light of the other cases we have reviewed, we might expect a rise in Islamic fundamentalism, coupled with a significant decline in the socio-economic fortunes of women, to be accompanied by a further marginalization of the role of *bomoh*. These would seem likely to be circumstances which would promote the development of a women's spirit cult, but with a corresponding feminization of spirit-inspired *bomohs*. More generally, where adorcism is apparently absent, the practise of exorcism may also be more complex and ambiguous than it appears initially. Thus (and this is not, apparently, the current situation in Malaysia) the same patients may repeatedly and regularly attend the same exorcistic rites, experiencing ecstatic possession on each occasion. This, for example, is reported in the North African cult of Islamic Saints (Ferchiou 1991) and in the celebrated contemporary Christian case of Archbishop Milingo's Catholic exorcistic ceremonies in Rome.[3] In such cases, repeated exorcism, although carried out in the name of the established, male-dominated religion seems paradoxically to stimulate and incorporate what amounts to an implicit ecstatic cult. Adorcism – the formal antithesis of exorcism – may, after all, not be so remote and may even be concealed within the same rites. Thus, if as I argue, exorcism is regularly employed, amongst other things, to control women and adorcism is not formally constituted, the latter, evidently, may break out subterraneously even *within* an exorcistic process itself.[4] This unexpected synthesis seems to me to represent a weaker challenge to, and a fuller endorsement of, established male religion than is the case with full-blown adorcism. Nevertheless, recognition of the fundamental ambiguity here, whether explicit or implicit, may increase the tendency for exorcists to be viewed as dangerously familiar with the powers which they regularly confront in the name of the orthodox faith.[5] This would help to explain the fundamentally ambiguous status of exorcists which is so marked in the examples discussed here – as well as elsewhere.

CHAPTER 8

The power of the past: African "survivals" in Islam

I

If the shaman triumphantly conquers and domesticates malign power and transmutes it into benign mystical energy (converting negative into positive charisma), his heroic role may still be exercised in a cult context, which in its wider external setting remains marginal and retains its negative aura of witchcraft and cannibalism. Marginality may be traced either spatially or temporally, and the two dimensions, as we shall see, are apt to interpenetrate and coalesce. This concluding chapter will argue that, in addition to providing a deeper and more accurate understanding of the *internal* dynamics of charismatic cults, our comparative analysis also illuminates the *external* significance of cults in the definition of ideological boundaries. Reconsidering in this wider context some of the cults discussed earlier, we thus achieve new insight into the meaning of "survivals" in religion (and of religious orthodoxy), taking the particular circumstances of African Islam to exemplify more general phenomena in world religions.

As with other world religions, elements of belief and practice that in a given Muslim setting are not officially recognized as part of international orthodoxy are generally assumed to represent local "survivals" from pre-Islamic times. Such assumptions about the persistence of unwelcome archaic elements from the past are by no means limited to the traditional religious elite. They are equally readily endorsed by modern scholars of religion. A characteristic example of this widespread view is found in a contemporary account of Tunisian popular Islam entitled "Survivances mystiques et culte de possession dans le maraboutisme Tunisien." The author, a Tunisian sociologist, presents maraboutism (the north African cult of saints and holy men) as the embodiment of two "systems of different values, asceticism and animism."[1] Maraboutism, we are told, derives from pre-Islamic north African roots, and its associated cult of possession is the means by which "ancient animist beliefs are perpetuated . . . In contact with Islam, the traditional 'spirits' are simply confounded with Muslim jinns and the veneration paid to sorcerers transferred to saints *awliya*" (Ferchiou: 48).

This interpretation, which ascribes pluralist tendencies in the contemporary practice of popular Islam to the pre-Islamic past, is naturally reinforced by those perennial currents of Islamic fundamentalism (recurrently manifested as "reformism") that condemn without qualification all forms of saintly mediation as heresy. At different times and places most Muslim cultures strongly suffused with mystical Sufism have not lacked for stern critics preaching such alternative Islamic fundamentalism. This antimystical puritanism has, in turn, fostered down-to-earth skepticism about the exaggerated powers attributed by the credulous to certain saints. If refined literary Sufism attracts these strictures, the florid possession cults readily seen as its vulgar popular expression invite violent denunciation as stubborn relics of "pre-Islamic superstition," such as might be found among recently converted pagans on the fringes of the House of Islam.

Puritan orthodoxy – or "scripturalism," as it is sometimes misleadingly called – and Sufi mysticism clearly represent diametrically different styles of Islamic religiosity. Do they then possess equally distinct social correlates? Western writers on Islam often assume so, this view being perhaps most trenchantly formulated in Ernest Gellner's "pendulum model" of Islam.[2] According to this theory, these styles reflect the theological chasm separating the literate well-informed *'ulama* (Muslim clerics) of the towns and their illiterate (or semiliterate) country cousins. The distinction follows the familiar contrast between "great" and "little" traditions emphasized so often in discussions of the other "world religions."

This interpretation seems to me inadequate. In its most basic terms, what is really at stake here is a broader issue: the fierce and constantly recharged theological debate concerning the interpretation of the Prophet's message. Here attention focuses on the meaning and importance of such famous revelatory passages in the Koran as the injunction to believers to "seek the means to come to Him" (v. 39), traditionally taken by Sufis to signal the mediatory power of saints. As the distinguished Arabist A. J. Arberry sums the matter up, in the history of Islam "the esoteric exposition of the Koran became a central point in the hard training of the Sufi."[3] In such circumstances rustic illiteracy could hardly be expected to be the necessary precondition for developing a Sufistic interpretation of Islam; indeed, rather the contrary. At the same time, what fundamentalist theologians and their unconscious sociological hagiologists, stereotypically represent as potentially heretical and certainly marginal – superstitious "pre-Islamic survivals" – possess a highly problematic quality. As I hope to demonstrate, phenomena characterized as "fringe" or "marginal" Islam are, on closer inspection, sometimes so intimately connected with "core" Islam that they seem part of a single complex. Moreover, what in a particular cultural context is regularly categorized as "pre-Islamic survival" is in many cases nothing of the sort.

II

The concept of "pre-Islamic survivals" is naturally consistent with a historical (not to say evolutionary) approach and is part of the well-documented process by which today's religion (or ideology) reduces yesterday's religion to the status of magic, each successive religious vogue marginalizing its predecessor. While this process obviously does take place, we have also to recall the alternative possibility in such religious dialogues – the synthesis or syncretism exemplified among the Bedouin

Arabs themselves[4] and among other "tribal" Islamic peoples
(e.g., the Somali)[5] in the transformation of local and clan
ancestors into Sufi saints. In the Muslim world generally,
pilgrimages to the shrines of such local saints are usually
known as the "poor man's *hajj*," thus making a direct equation
with pilgrimage to Mecca. Both processes (marginalization
and syncretism) may occur at the same time – some elements
of an earlier religion being marginalized (as evil *jinns* or
sorcery, *sihir*) while others are assimilated as saints. As our
earlier discussion suggests (Chapter 4), spirit-possession cults
in Islamic cultures provide a convenient and revealing context
for examining these various possible accommodations.

Such cults are regularly presented as being based upon
pre-Islamic survivals. Thus, as we have seen, the West African
bori cult (Chapter 7) is generally treated in the literature as
representing the religion of the pre-Islamic Hausa, displaced
by Islam and thrust into a shadowy, peripheral position in a
male-dominated Muslim society.[6] A similar pattern emerges
with greater clarity in the case of the formerly matrilineal
Zaramo of Tanzania, where the adoption of Islam has
apparently weakened the position of women, who seek redress
through possession cults involving traditional (as well as
modern) spirits.[7]

Although these cults tend to be presented negatively in the
Islamic settings where they flourish and to appeal particularly
to women, low status men, and marginal people generally,
their position is fundamentally ambiguous. Some at least
of the spirits involved are readily subsumed under those
mentioned in the Koran and so are scripturally legitimated;
others are even considered to be Muslim. Again, although
the rituals associated with them are regularly described in the
literature as "exorcisms," the adequacy and accuracy of
this characterization can be questioned since treatment
frequently entails recurrent rituals and in effect initiation into
specialized cults (cf. Chapter 6). What is really involved is, in
fact, often a kind of conversion.

Recognition of this crucial fact opens the door to a deeper
understanding of the problem of syncretism and survival in

African Islam (and no doubt in Islam elsewhere as well). The standard approach to the dissemination of Islam in Africa follows the classic diffusionist model, whose three stages are described by the leading British authority, J. S. Trimingham,[8] as "germination," "crisis," and "gradual reorientation." From a similar but more specifically theological perspective, H. J. Fisher[9] has recently proposed an analogous Van Gennepian tripartite formula involving "quarantine," "mixing," and "reform."

III

Although such cultural diffusion models are clearly valuable, it is also important to examine how socioeconomic changes create conditions favoring the adoption of Islam (and in other contexts, the other "world religions").[10] A critical consideration here is the scope that Islam offers as a viable personal and universalistic group identity when socioeconomic changes are expanding social and experiential horizons.

In this context, the flamboyant, ecstatic conversion experience of which so much is made in Christianity (both historically and currently, in charismatic circles) has, I believe, been overlooked in Islam – or at least in African Islam, where a number of suggestive cases have been reported. In west Africa, for example, among the Mossi who are in the process of becoming Muslims, barrenness in pagan women may be diagnosed by diviners as a sign that potential children refuse to be born except as Muslims. Conversion to Islam is the obvious remedy (Skinner 1966: 360).

This "therapeutic" route to the faith is certainly in evidence among the Giriama of Kenya, traditional subsistence cultivators trading with the Muslim Swahili and Arabs of the east African coast. Beginning in the 1920s, as they began to emulate their neighbors in producing cash crops, a new entrepreneurial class came into existence among this people. These successful traders attracted the envy of their less well-favoured kinsmen and were evidently "in the market" for protection against such mystical aggression. Some found asylum by adopting Christianity (in the spirit of the Protestant ethic, according to Weber and Tawney); and others became Muslims. The way in which this happened is quite apposite: Members of this nascent class fell victim to illnesses that were diagnosed as caused by Muslim spirits for which the only secure remedy was conversion to Islam. Such "therapeutic Muslims" had, of course, been called to Islam, involuntarily, by an illness for which they could not be held accountable. They had not sought this; it had happened against their will. But the consequences are revealing. The adoption of Islam, with its various dietary requirements, freed these upwardly mobile privileged individuals from certain traditional communal obligations. At the same time, it protected them against mystical attack and provided them with the higher status Swahili-style Islamic identity that suited their economic activities and ambitions.[11]

This appeal of Muslim therapeutic techniques, and indeed of Islam itself as a mystical defense system has, I think, been underestimated in analyzing the expansion of Islam in sub-Saharan Africa. In the present context, however, my concern is to emphasize how Muslims may be recruited by a process which in other circumstances would smack of unorthodox deviance or of flamboyant fringe maraboutism. An even more instructive if more complex case, perhaps, is the cult of Sheikh Hussein of Bale in southern Ethiopia. Sheikh Hussein, whose origins appear to go back to the thirteenth century and who is thus, in effect, the spiritual residue of the ancient Muslim state of Bale, has become in effect the patron saint of Muslims in Ethiopia. The annual festival at the shrine attracts great numbers of pilgrims from places as far distant as northern and central Ethiopia, northern Kenya, and southern Somalia. Sheikh Hussein has connections with the Somali coast and, more generally, with the inter-riverine area of southern Somalia, where an elaborate complex of shrines dedicated to the saint replicates the parent pilgrim center in Bale.[12]

In its contemporary form in Bale, where there has been a complex succession of ethnic migrations over the centuries, this Islamic cult has come to embody prominent features from the traditional religion of the Oromo peoples who invaded the region in the sixteenth century. The Oromo, it must be appreciated, are Cushitic speakers like the Somali, to whom they are closely related ethnically and historically. Sheikh Hussein's cult has thus been to a degree "Oromo-ized" by the accretion of cultural elements that are *post-* rather than *pre-*Islamic. Indeed its constituent elements have been successively de- and re-Islamicized in what is by no means a unique process in the history of such religious movements. As has long been recognized, the cult's wide-ranging appeal in an Ethiopia dominated by Semitic-speaking Christians owes much to this syncretic character, blending Islamic and Oromo symbols and projecting an Islamic identity that today subsumes and transmutes traditional Oromo values on a pattern influenced by the Somali Muslim prototype.

This synthetic Muslim identity has assumed a pervasive spiritual character that extends far beyond Sheikh Hussein's shrine and those who make pilgrimages there. In northern Kenya, where it has penetrated widely (apparently quite recently), Sheikh Hussein's cult has assumed an active missionary role in the form, as its devotees see it, of a Sufi mystical religious order known as Husseiniya. In the small township of Isiolo, with its ethnically mixed Cushitic and Nilo-Hamitic population, in competition with Christianity the Sheikh's cult is especially prominent among the local Cushitic groups. Recruitment to the "brotherhood" frequently follows illness and affliction, treated by initiation into the syncretic cult and the adoption or confirmation of Islamic identity. Membership appeals particularly to "poor, destitute Borana (a branch of the Oromo) and Somali" – especially destitute pastoralists who have lost their livestock in war and famine and drifted into Isiolo district headquarters seeking a means of survival (Hjort 1979: 42). There are a higher proportion of Borana (Oromo) men than Somali men in the cult, which despite its Somali connections in Ethiopia is viewed by the local Somali Islamic establishment in northern Kenya as "primitive" and "satanic" – a kind of intrusive spiritual malaise "picked up from the bush." Cult adherents are even forbidden to enter the mosque. This negative view is shared by the Kenyan administrative authorities, who apparently regard the flamboyant popular rituals as encouraging political and social discontent – to which, in all probability, the rites are actually a harmless, palliative reaction. Sternly condemned in the mosque by the orthodox Somali sheikhs (usually members of the Qadariya or Salihiya religious orders), the cult is nevertheless warmly supported by their wives. This is an interesting but by no means unusual example of sex-linked religious pluralism with close analogies to the Tunisian situation, to which we shall return presently. For the moment, however, let us simply note here that what the women embrace and the men discard as "pre-Islamic superstition" is something much more complicated than this dismissive categorization implies.

IV

In southern Somalia, to which we now turn, Sheikh Hussein's cult exists alongside the more pervasive and widely known *zar* cult (*sar* in Somali),[13] which we have already encountered in Chapter 3. If, in this context, the Husseiniya might tendentiously be claimed to subsume local pre-Islamic "survivals" (inasmuch as there is a pre-Islamic Oromo ethnic substratum in the population of southern Somalia), this is emphatically out of the question with regard to the *sar* possession cult. In its Somali form, there is no evidence that the word *sar* refers to a local pre-Islamic spirit or ritual. On the contrary, the term conveys the idea of extraneous or external origin and is associated with Ethiopia, whence what is generally considered the most dangerous variety of spirit intrusion (*mengis*, from Amharic "government") clearly derives.[14] As we have seen in Chapter 3, there is a striking prevalence of women victims, which has generally been interpreted as reflecting the frustrations associated with their subordinate position in a male-dominated culture.[15]

As we can now see more clearly than before, the *sar* possession cult among Somali women is primarily an urban rather than a rural phenomenon. Although men are the dominant sex in the social system of Somali pastoral nomads, women, charged with the management of small stock, enjoy considerable freedom and never wear the veil. It is only in towns that women are sometimes veiled,[16] and it is precisely in such urban contexts that possession flourishes. This contrast fits neatly with the male accusation that the spirits – which men are apt to condemn and regard skeptically – attack the wives of the rich more often than those of the poor, treatment being an expensive business and tyically adding (as we have seen) to the afflicted wife's wardrobe of costly clothes and personal jewelry. Although the exploited husbands denounce the cult as "primitive superstition," it is striking that the women most deeply involved are actually not hard-pressed nomads of the bush but, on the contrary, relatively prosperous members of the new urban population, wearing modern dresses and living in homes, equipped, in addition to servants, with radios, tape recorders, and refrigerators.[17] Perhaps the most severe frustration for those who have not yet been liberated in a modern sense, through education and extra-domestic employment, is boredom.

A recent study of the incidence of cases interpreted in the same *zar* idiom in Egypt is revealing in this respect.[18] In the intensively cultivated Nile Delta, *zar* cult involvement is more prominent in the lives of rich village leaders and landowners than in those of poor *fellahin* peasants. This is directly linked to constraints imposed by Islamic respectability on well-to-do wives, who are more homebound and dependent than their peasant counterparts. The latter enjoy greater economic and domestic independence, more freedom of movement, and stronger kin support. The richer women are more confined and cut off and correspondingly more intensely involved in expensive *zar* cult rituals, which their husbands pay for. Whatever cross-sexual tensions may be ventilated here, there is also a significant element of conspicuous consumption, as wives test and demonstrate the resources of their spouses (cf. Wilson 1967). Peasant women tend to be only occasionally attacked by *zar* spirits, at times of exceptional strain and difficulty, and are less likely to be drawn into formal cult membership and long-term (i.e., perpetual) cult activity.

The pattern in the neighboring Sudan is similar.[19] *Zar*, which as usual is viewed as an intrusive foreign influence, is essentially an urban bourgeois phenomenon, ensconced in the bosom of respectable, traditionalist Muslim families. At the upper end of the spirit catchment many of the women involved are married to prominent men, including religious dignitaries, who while denouncing *zar* as pagan idolatry are not above asking their wives to consult the cult leaders on their behalf. Again we find that the most keen adherents are women with rich husbands – prosperous merchants, butchers, contractors, goldsmiths. And, notwithstanding the controversy it evokes, *zar* programs have been staged on Sudanese television.

While some of the terminology employed in the rituals of this Sudanese women's *zar* cult directly parallels that used in marriage ceremonies, it is difficult not to be struck by the obvious similarities between this women's movement and the men's Sufi brotherhoods. Like the *tariqas*, the *zar* groups celebrate all the major Islamic festivals, and no rituals are held in the month of Ramadan. They begin and end their proceedings with prayers in honor of the Prophet Muhammad; their leaders,[20] who regularly go on pilgrimages to Mecca, are called *sheikhas* (female sheikhs) and like their male Sufi counterparts are said "to know the way" (that the faithful should follow). In both cases, the position of leader may be ascribed (by birth) or achieved (by initiation). Again, in the Sufi rituals men achieve states of ecstasy which (even if they differ in style and tempo) invite comparison to the women's possession trances in the *zar* cult.

The Sudanese pantheon of *zar* spirits, moreover, is headed by the "holy saints" – the founders of the brotherhoods traditionally so important in the lives of men. These are followed by other groups: the "Ethiopians"; the "Pashas"; the "Arabs" (representative of the nomadic Sudanese tribes); the "Europeans and Christians" – including Jews, Copts,

Greeks, Armenians, French, and British (specifically General Gordon and Lord Cromer); the "ladies or daughters," associated with the prestigious "holy saints"; the "blacks" (from the south); the Fellata; and various other categories. These constitute loose general categories that readily admit new accretions. Thus for a time socialist soldier spirits made their appearance, and more recently Gamal Abdel Nasser and the Saudi OPEC oil minister Sheik Yamani are reported to have entered the seance galaxy.[21] The *zar* spirit repertoire is evidently a fluid historical mirror of the world of male Sudanese experience.

v

While certain notorious non-Islamic historical figures – such as General Gordon and Lord Cromer – thus appear to have had immortality thrust upon them, in general the historical identity of the spirits involved clearly makes it difficult to classify this Sudanese possession cult as a straightforward survival or local pre-Islamic phenomenon. The same objection is obviously even more pertinent when we consider the wider geographical distribution of the *zar* cult along the east African littoral (and islands), in Egypt, North Africa, and along the Arabian peninsula to Iran. Although sometimes known under other names, throughout this vast area the cult retains its Ethiopian associations and attracts women generally, along with peripheral male immigrants from Somalia and the east African coast who are treated as second-class citizens by those Arabian and Iranian employers whom they serve, often in low-status occupations. As with its Sudanese version, this complex of possession cults involving Muslim and non-Muslim spirits, holy men, and pagans, seems generally to attract women of higher social position than its male adherents.[22] This is consistent with the more strict segregation of women in orthodox bourgeois circles, as noted earlier in relation to the Egyptian *fellahin*.

Although possibly in some places subsuming other genuinely indigenous local spirits[23] ("authentic survivals"), it is generally accepted that the *zar* cult has spread by diffusion from Ethiopia. This process is assumed to have accompanied the slave trade from Ethiopia and the east African coast in the late eighteenth and early nineteenth centuries and the subsequent settlement in the Arabian peninsula of African migrant workers. Indeed, the evidence currently available suggests that *zar* only began to assume prominence in Egypt in the second half of the nineteenth century, or even later.[24]

More generally, it appears that it was in this relatively recent period that *zar* spirits began to diffuse widely outside their spiritual headquarters (if not homeland) in the Gondar region of Ethiopia, where they possessed both Christian and Muslim Ethiopians. Gondar is historically the center of Christian Ethiopia and of the fusion between its Cushitic and Semitic cultures and religions. Its ecumenical spiritual pantheon thus also directly reflects this complex legacy, and it is striking to note that in this official bastion of Ethiopian Christianity the Arabic word "saint" (*weli*) is used interchangeably with the Amharic *zar*, and the leaders of *zar* cult groups are frequently referred to as "masters" (*bala*) of "saints" (*awliya*).

By analogy with other comparable "peripheral spirit cults" (see Chapter 3), it would probably be more accurate to speak of the diffusion (and rediffusion) of *zar* spirits rather than of an undifferentiated *zar* cult.[25] The dispersal of the spirits would then presumably be associated with increasingly intensive relations between the countries and peoples of the Nile and the Horn of Africa during the Anglo-Egyptian administration of the Sudan and the ensuing *mahdiya* – at which time, Michel Leiris's informants in Gondar recalled,[26] a new class of militant Tigrean spirits known as *kabere* (from *keber*, pride, honor) began to possess people. This is surely also what the presence of the Pashas and of General Gordon and Lord Cromer in the Sudanese *zar* pantheon suggests. It is equally in accord with Leiris's observation that in Gondar one is especially likely to catch (or be caught by) *zar* through a chance encounter with a possessed person in a market. The pilgrimage to Mecca (whither the *zar* cult was also carried) was doubtless also a major vehicle in the wider spread of these, and many other, concepts and ideas.

However, the demonstration of effective connections and lines of communication for the potential spread of ideas (and cult practices) does not explain why they arose in their particular places of origin when they did, nor why they appealed to other sections of society in the centers to which they were carried. The latter explanation is to be found, I believe, as suggested earlier, in the special circumstances of those most prone to the attentions of these intrusive spirits. Frequently those concerned are marginal male migrants of non-Arab origin, and more generally, Muslim women – especially where an intensification of conservative orthodoxy further weakens the position and rights of women.[27]

It is tempting to speculate that the wider dissemination of *zar* in and from Ethiopia in the nineteenth century might be connected with the expansion and consolidation of the Christian Amhara empire under Menelik during this period. (This would be in harmony with the militaristic character attributed in Gondar to the *zar* spirits and with the emphasis placed on hunting and fighting motifs in the cult imagery). Beyond that, while discounting the "demonstration effect" as a necessary and sufficient explanation for the *diffusion* of new ideas, I do not think we should entirely ignore the factor of fashion. This again is clearly linked to the question of identity and status and to the manner in which perennial aspirations are aired and expressed.

It is unnecessary to discuss the parallel and, in north Africa, sometimes overlapping *bori* cult in comparable detail (see Chapter 3). Certainly its diffusion from its native northern Nigeria and Niger is directly associated with the trans-Saharan slave trade and with African settlement amongst the local Arab and Berber populations of the Magreb. Even without such population movements, the trans-Saharan trading connections could well have prompted the influx of intrusive *bori* spirits to Islamic north Africa. Be that as it may, and whatever its original status amongst the Hausa, the fact is that in Arab north Africa the *bori* cult is obviously no more a bona fide pre-Islamic "survival" than its *zar* counterpart. It is thus highly appropriate that we should find references to *bori* spirits in Sudanese *zar* contexts (where the two words are sometimes used interchangeably), and to *zar* spirits in north African *bori* contexts. It is typical and equally apposite that the ambiguous possession cult siren Lalla "Aisha,"[28] who figures prominently in both regions, should be known in the Sudan as "the Maghrebi" and in Morocco as "the Sudani"! The traffic in spirits is almost as widespread and intensive as the teaching of Islam.

VI

With the examples of the *zar* and *bori* cults I have sought to demonstrate that, in the settings in which they flourish, these are far from representing genuine pre-Islamic "survivals." If, as in some cases they and their analogues may be, they are somewhere ultimately of pre-Islamic origin, then what we find here is a continuous process of reactive counterdiffusion; as the spirit of Islam flows in one direction, other spirits return the compliment, as it were. So religious phenomena that existed before Islam entered a given region, and which are there authentically "pre-Islamic," become after their diffusion to other Islamic areas post- and sometimes even pan-Islamic. Religious currents in the Islamic metropolis are thus in constant dynamic tension with those on the periphery.[29]

Hence, although orthodox fundamentalist Islam stands at one end of the spectrum, with magical maraboutism at the other, these opposed religious styles cannot be unambiguously identified with the dichotomies between town and tribe, literate and illiterate, and so on. The first, if it does not actually entail at least tends to provoke the second as a supplement and appendix. It is not just that the marginal ritual practices of women mirror the men's saints' cult, there being as Sophie Ferchiou (1972: 48–64) puts it a distinctive male and female religious "comportment" in Islam. More is involved than simply a restrained male style of religiosity counterpoised by a flamboyant female mode. The burden of religious orthodoxy is depicted as falling primarily to men as the pilgrims and pillars of Islam, whose religious devotions count also for their womenfolk, who are thereby exempted from an equivalent degree of direct religiosity. From this perspective, with their Islamic embroidery, the women's possession cults seem to represent a kind of vicarious participation in the male-dominated Islamic sanctuary. My own alternative perspective suggests that the ecstatic women's cults have a direct appeal precisely to the wives of the more orthodox men – the models of Islamic respectability – while indirectly offering the latter the privilege of vicarious participation in what they ostensibly condemn as superstition and heresy. Thus, if there is a dual spiritual economy, its two branches are interdependent and complementary.

More generally, sociologists of Islam regularly attack Arabists and Orientalists for taking Islam literally, as it is presented in the Koran, rather than as it is expressed in the beliefs of living Muslims who interpret the Koran as they see fit. They, however, are also prone to present the "big tradition" view of Islam as the "religion of the book," treating supposed deviations as manifestations of rustic illiteracy and ignorance. This ignores the striking fact that the vast corpus of written sayings attributed to the Prophet (*hadith*) and interpretations broadcast from urban centers of Muslim excellence is regularly accompanied by an equally extensive *written* apparatus of magical and astrological Islamic lore. The latter not only provides an Islamic base and legitimation for local pre-Islamic mystical beliefs and rituals but actually sometimes introduces such "magical" beliefs where they did not previously exist. Indeed, as has recently been observed in Malaysia, "a growing Islamic fervour is equally balanced by an increasing interest in magic" (Wazir-Jahan Karim 1981: 204; 1990, 1992).

It is important to establish what is happening here. It is not just oral, pre-Islamic culture that dilutes the unswerving eternal truths conserved in literate mainstream Islam. Elements in literate mainstream Islam also introduce and perpetuate alternative renderings of the Prophet's message.

Islam is thus not the "religion of the book" but, rather, the "religion of the books," a package of written compendia that in their catholic profusion facilitate the diffusion and rediffusion of so-called pre-Islamic survivals.

This reappraisal of the meaning of the concept of "survival" in the context of a world religion emphasizes once again the importance of accurately contextualizing beliefs, which was stressed in the opening chapter. The official picture of what does and does not constitute ideological orthodoxy is the officially constructed picture, molding and remolding the "past" to provide an effective backdrop for the revealed truth of the present. In this process the invention of antitradition is just as important as the invention of tradition. Thus what in terms of establishment values is marginal to society, and correspondingly charged with ambiguous negative power, becomes marginal in time – an anachronistic survival from the past.

The sinister power of the past attributed to these marginal cults of affliction generally, and particularized in the person of the shaman, includes dark allusions to witchcraft and cannibalism. Religious survivals, in the shape of marginal charismatic cults, thus bring together all those outwardly negative facets of mystical power that I have been arguing in this book are better understood as permutations of the same underlying phenomenon than as autonomous "things." Religious phenomena, of course, lend themselves exceedingly well to reification; and one of the main obstacles to progress in understanding here is the reluctance of so many anthropologists to submit such material to searching, empirically grounded analysis along the lines proposed in this book.

Notes

1: ANTHROPOLOGICAL FIELDWORK AND THE CONTEXT OF BELIEF

1 See the pamphlet *Department of Anthropology 1972–73* (London School of Economics, 1972), p. 4.
2 For an interesting analysis of the first edition of this British anthropologists' *Who's Who*, see E. and S. Ardener (1965: 295–314).
3 See, for example, Leach (1970).
4 Lévi-Strauss (1977, vol. 1: 328).
5 Lévi-Strauss (1977, vol. 1: 332).
6 Lévi-Strauss (1977, vol. 1: 337).
7 See Richards (1967: 286–98) and Fardon, 1990.
8 Mead (1972: 121).
9 Rosemary Firth (1972: 10–32).
10 See, e.g., Casagrande, ed. (1960: xi); Lévi-Strauss (1977, vol. 1: 373); and Freilich, ed. (1970: 13). In Freilich (1970) see also p. 35, where it is recommended that preparation for fieldwork include some training in psychotherapy.
11 Rosemary Firth (1972: 31).
12 Evans-Pritchard (1951: 77–9).
13 See, e.g., Casagrande (1960: xi), and Freilich (1970: 13), and for an admirably comprehensive discussion Ellen (1984). Historiographically, as the actual practise of in-depth, scholarly fieldwork has declined (partly due to financial constraints and to security problems), the practise of writing about it has exploded exponentially. Under the beguiling inspiration of post-modernist trends in literary studies and the culturally relative anthropology fashionable in America in the 1980s, a torrent of self-conscious, largely repetitious, and ultimately stultifying writing has expatiated on the textual status of ethnography (thereby giving a curious new meaning to the staid pedagogic reading list sense

of "ethnographic texts"). For representative texts of this inherently self-destructive (but regrettably persistent) discourse, see Clifford and Marcus 1986; Marcus and Fischer 1986; Sanjek 1990; and Crapanzano 1992. Useful critical assessments of this "metatwaddle" (Gellner 1992) can be found in Kuper 1994 and Reyna 1994.

14 For this analogy I owe much to conversations with Dr. Peter Fry, who I think perceived the parallel before I did. This view of anthropological fieldwork, as a shamanic quest, is aptly deployed by Roy Rappaport (1986) in his lively assessment of the Freeman controversy concerning the accuracy of Margaret Mead's Samoan ethnography.

15 It is thus not surprising that so many of those who write in this vein are Americans.

16 See, e.g., the very revealing final volume of the monumental *Mythologiques, L'Homme nu* (Lévi-Strauss 1971), particularly pp. 559–621.

17 Robert Murphy (1972: 24).

18 We must notice, however, that Lowie himself explains in the preface to the 1937 edition of *Primitive Society* (first edition: 1920) that he intended the phrase to convey his own disillusionment with Western civilization in the wake of the First World War.

19 Especially in those articles republished as the first part of *Anthropologie structurale*.

20 See Forge (1972).

21 Gluckman (1963: 35).

22 Stanner, in Casagrande (1960: 85).

23 V. W. Turner (1960: 335–7).

24 Griaule (1965: 220). For a perceptive recent "Anglophone" assessment of Griaule's contribution, see J. Clifford (1983: 121–56). See also van Beek 1991; de Heusch 1991.

25 Lévi-Strauss (1970: 13).

26 Douglas (1957: 46–57). The anomalous fact that there are *two* Lele pangolins, only one of which is the object of a cult, is discussed in the following chapter.

27 V. W. Turner (1967: 13).

28 Evans-Pritchard (1965: 24–7).

29 Raymond Firth (1960: 17).

30 Lienhardt (1961).

31 Griaule (1965: 37).

32 Kiev (1972: 171–2).

33 See, e.g., Thomas (1971) and Macfarlane (1970).

34 Evans-Pritchard (1937).

35 I. M. Lewis (1971).

36 This interpretation goes back at least as far as Kluckhohn's *Navaho Witchcraft* (1944) and is echoed in such recent surveys as Lucy Mair (1960) and Harrington and Whiting (1972: 469–508). Cf. also Marwick (1970: 280–95).

37 Leach (1966: 39–50). See also Spiro (1968: 242–61) and correspondence in *Man* (1968: 311–13, 651–6; 1969: 132–4).

38 Raymond Firth (1966: 1–17) and Evans-Pritchard (1966: 398). See also Evans-Pritchard (1956) and Littlejohn (1970: 91–114).

39 Not, however, in my view for the reasons advanced in Rodney Needham's distillation of the opinions of the Oxford linguistic philosophers (Needham 1972). I find Ernest Gellner's "Concepts and Society" (1962) more helpful in diagnosing the anthropologist's obsessional tendency to treat all exotic beliefs as equally coherent and cogent, thus making it difficult to recognize significant inconsistencies. See also Gustav Jahoda's very interesting comments on some of the issues involved here from the standpoint of a social psychologist (Jahoda [1970a: 33–50]). See also Jahoda (1970b: 115–30; 1971).

40 See Douglas (1970).

41 See Gilbert A. Lewis (1975). Dr. Lewis employs Venn diagrams to summarize the variables involved in the selection of explanations for illness as these are advanced in actual case histories. This provides an admirably succinct method of presenting complex data and could be used to collect and store directly comparable material. If this methodological innovation were widely adopted and applied with sufficient sensitivity and discrimination, it might even in time lead to the establishment of quantifiable differences in explanatory systems.

2: THE SPIRIT SPIDER AND THE PANGOLIN

1 Thus, for example, Hadfield (1969: 193–4) claims that the spider as a symbol, with its soft squashy body and projecting limbs, is an objectification of the soft, nauseating feelings produced after an orgasm, starting in the solar plexus and spreading out to the other parts of the abdomen and body like the legs of the spider.

2 According to Biebuyck (1953) there are in fact three varieties of pangolin in this area of the Congo, but only two – *Manis tricuspis* and *Manis gigantea* – are common.

3 See the article "Pangolin" in Haltenorth and Diller (1980).

4 Thus, according to de Heusch, Lega pangolin symbolism is driven by sociological forces, whereas among the Lele "cosmogonic"

determinants select the small pangolin in preference to the large pangolin. This seems a quite arbitrary analytical judgement for which no convincing justification is offered. A more satisfactory line of explanation would seek determining factors of the same order (sociological or cosmological) in each case. Thus, as I argue below, the varying prominence of the two pangolins in the Congolese societies discussed in this article *may* reflect cosmological differences in these cultures (see also Zuesse 1979).

5 This assertion seems to contradict the Komo classification of the small and large pangolins with the porcupine, Gambian rat and the aardvark as "burrowing animals" (de Mahieu 1980: 36) within the class of quadrupeds.

6 The pangolin's anthropomorphic links are also acknowledged by the Ma'Betsiek, a Malay aboriginal group, but in a slightly different way. In this case, the pangolin (*manis javanica*) is said to have formed from human after-births. The after-birth is buried in the ground wrapped in a mat which is considered to resemble the pangolin's scales (Begum Karim 1981: 48).

7 In fact, the pangolin's reaction, like the hedgehog's, is defensive and is accompanied by the emission of an unpleasant smell.

8 In his short monograph on Sotho cosmology, citing Douglas, Hammond-Tooke (1981: 133–4) similarly explains the mystical properties of the local pangolin (*Manis teminckii* – which has the same habits as *manis gigantea*, the pangolin which is *not* ritually prominent among the Lele!). "Few animals" he states "can be as anomalous as the pangolin. It is a four legged, claw-footed mammal, but it is covered with scales like a fish, looks like a reptile and bears its young singly as humans usually do." With these diverse characteristics, the pangolin has an "anomalous position" in the local system of zoological classification and hence is endowed with "tremendous power." In the absence of other evidence (for example on linkages with spirits), this explains, according to Hammond-Tooke, the prominence of the pangolin as a kind of royal game to be handed over to a chief if killed in hunting by a commoner, and as a source of chiefly medicine. It so happens that the name of the tribe studied here also means pangolin, but Hammond-Tooke says that this is "fortuitous."

Similarly (if more in accordance with my emphasis on its positive power) among the Sherbo, MacCormack argues that "the pangolin is highly anomalous in terms of Sherbo thought categories, and is therefore a powerful symbol of mediation between the categories . . . it mediates the three cosmological tiers, from deep ancestral water to the sky which trees penetrate." The pangolin in question here is *Manis tricuspis* (MacCormack 1980: 116).

9 Admission to the prestigious Lele Pangolin cult is restricted to men of one of the founding clans of the village, with fathers also from a founding clan, and with wives belonging to a founding clan. Thus the pangolin seems to be tightly associated with local *endogamy* rather than with *exogamy* as Douglas claims (see also de Heusch 1985: 36).

10 For Douglas's and de Heusch's response to these criticisms, see Douglas 1993: 161–4; de Heusch 1993: 159–61; and for my reply, Lewis 1993: 165–6. See also Fardon 1993: 361–3; and Lewis 1993: 363.

3: POSSESSION CULTS IN CONTEXT

1 For an admirably comprehensive bibliography of works published prior to 1950, see Bouteiller (1950: 327–65); for more recent material, see Zaretsky and Shambaugh (1978).

2 Cf. Firth's wide-ranging discussion of the effects and implications of the observer's personal bias in religious sociology (Firth 1959).

3 White suggests that the high incidence of these possession afflictions among Luvale women is, in this context, connected with the practice of virilocal marriage, which separates a wife from her natal kin and prevents her from regularly participating in offerings made to her own ancestors (White 1961: 48). These spirit-possession afflictions have thus had the effect of reminding women of their kin allegiances and thereby helping to maintain matrilineal solidarity.

4 For a fuller discussion see Lewis (1969).

5 The transition from the rigid traditional attitude to the modern explicit recognition of love is clearly shown in many of the poems of Ilmi Bownderi (c. 1908–38) who is generally regarded as the first major Somali poet to compose works in the classical style treating this theme directly. The following lines addressed to the woman he loved but who would not marry him refer directly to the forms of possession discussed here:

> Rapt in deceitful trance, I thought that I was sleeping with her,
> But it was only a jinn counterfeiting her image,
> I tried to catch her by the hand, but the place beside me was
>   empty.
> When I discovered that it was alone I was striving,

> I woke up abruptly, having tossed from side to side,
> And like a prowling lion, I rumpled my bed clothes,
> Attacking and pounding them, as if it were they who had caused
>   my deprivation
> And like a hero against whom men have combined to oppose, I
>   covered my face,
> I was humbled like the boy who, guarding his people's camels,
>   has them seized from him,
> I felt disgraced like a women to whom the words "I divorce you"
>   had been spoken,
> It is degrading to yearn for what you cannot have,
> Alas, alas, how disaster has overtaken me.
>
> [Abdillah and Andrzejewski, 1967]

6 Following Trimingham (1959: 31ff.) I use the word "cleric" as a general term for various Muslim holy men and religious functionaries who, though not necessarily part of any ecclesiastical hierarchy, figure so prominently in all Islamic societies.

7 For fuller details on the procedure of exorcism see Lewis (1969).

8 There are obvious analogies here with such exotic phenomena as the so-called "*Wiitiko* psychosis" found amongst Cree and Ojibwa Indians in the northern forestland of Canada. Like the Somali camel boys' *sar*, this affliction mainly affects men, and in this case those who have spent long periods alone in the frozen forest in an unsuccessful quest for food (Parker 1960: 603). Whatever its psychological status, this appears to be a parallel cultural phenomenon, associated with physical and social isolation and deprivation, and explained in terms of possession by a monster spirit called *Wiitiko*.

9 For accounts of these in the Sudan and north Africa, see Tremearne (1914) and Westermarck (1926).

10 The best published sources for the *bori* cults are Tremearne (1913; 1914), Greenberg (1946), Mary Smith (1954), and M. G. Smith (1957; 1962). See also below, Chapter 8.

11 Michael Onwuejeogwu, personal communication. I am also grateful for helpful comments from F. W. Parsons and Malam Esa of the School of Oriental and African Studies, London.

12 Wallace (1961) argues that Arctic hysteria (in some areas called *pibloktoq*) is the result of calcium deficiency in the Eskimo diet. This view, however, does not satisfactorily account for the differential sex incidence of the affliction. Wallace's assertion that the syndrome is not explained by the Eskimos themselves in terms of spirit-possession appears to contradict the evidence presented by Czaplicka and other authorities.

13 Colson (1969).

14 Cf. Leach (1961) and Lewis (1965).

15 Wallace (1959) has most interestingly argued that prevailing trends in psychotherapy may be related to sociocultural factors. In social systems with a "high level of organization" the emphasis in therapy tends to be on expressive catharsis, whereas in those with a "low level of organization" the bias is toward control therapy (with ego or superego reinforcement). Thus, according to Wallace, in traditional Iroquois society prior to 1650 therapy was mainly of the expressive kind associated with shamanistic rituals. Two hundred years later, however, after the misery and dislocation associated with colonization, the emphasis had shifted toward "control" psychotherapy associated with puritanical prophetic movements in which confession played an important part.

16 See, e.g., Fortes (1959), Horton (1961), and Wallace (1961: 281ff.).

17 Prominent among modern synoptic treatments of the subject are Thrupp (1962) and Lanternari (1963).

18 For a recent study of shamanistic practices associated with healing in rural France see Bouteiller (1950: 1999–248) and in rural Italy, Penna (1963).

19 See Shepherd *et al.* (1964) and Shepherd (1981). This differential sex incidence is also evident, though less extreme, in the registrar general's figures for hospitalization in cases of mental illness in England. On the basis of the 1959 figures, Little (1965) has calculated expectancy rates indicating that 7.4 percent of men and 11.1 percent of women can expect to be admitted to a mental hospital for treatment once during their lives. The most striking modern Western analogy to spirit possession, as some psychiatrists have realized, is, of course, Multiple Personality Disorder which assumed epidemic proportions in the USA in the 1980s. Ninety per cent of those so diagnosed are women who routinely recount 'memories' of having been sexually abused in childhood or, more colorfully, of having been abducted by Aliens. See Ross 1989; Schnabel 1995.

4: WITCHCRAFT WITHIN AND WITHOUT

1 Although very little is generally known of the history of peripheral possession cults in traditional societies, most observers of these cults, at least in Africa, report that they have arisen within this century. Since (almost invariably) they predominantly involve women and clearly operate to some extent as

women's protest movements, it seems probable that they reflect changing aspirations and attitudes toward their traditional status on the part of women. Thus, as the character of the spirits themselves suggests, they seem to be responses to social change and perhaps often direct reactions to the diffusion of modern views on the social role of women. Certainly, contrary to Wilson's unconvincing assertions concerning the allegedly complete socialization of women in traditional roles (Wilson 1967), in many cases there is direct evidence of spirit-possessed women seeking to assume male roles – roles that they specifically covet and their exclusion from which they explicitly resent. For particularly clear evidence of this see Harris (1957).

2 For a detailed discussion see Beattie (1969).

3 Cf. R. Turner (1970).

5: THE CANNIBAL'S CAULDRON

1 See Dubb, ed. (1960: 145ff.). For an extremely interesting, detailed account of popular ideas of vampirism, associated with fire-brigades, blood, and the color red in colonial east Africa, see White 1994.

2 Arab sources have indeed claimed that during the Crusades, Christian forces actually practiced cannibalism, eating their defeated foes as a final act of humiliation. (See Maalouf 1984.)

3 Professor Chavunduka is also president of the Zimbabwe National Healers Association (ZINATHA), formed with the collaboration of the minister of health in 1980.

4 In contrast, in post-colonial Africa, witchcraft is taken very seriously, and it is the witches (rather than witchdoctors) who are prosecuted in the courts. See, e.g., Geschiere and Fisig 1994. For interesting treatments of these themes by contemporary east African writers see Grace Ogot's novel *Land Without Thunder* and Alumidi Osinya's *Field Marshall Abdulla Salim Fisi (or How the Hyena Got His!)*. In the latter work, an Orwellian account of the recent history of Uganda, Amin and his ethnic supporters are depicted as hyenas who successfully wrest power from the leopards (Obote's people) who rule the game park (= Uganda). Forbidden by their leader to eat other animals, the hungry leopards are clandestinely supplied with human corpses by their friends the whites. The hyena regime quickly reverses this "animal law" and takes advantage of the devastations caused by a severe drought in the park, which makes large numbers of enfeebled animals easy prey for the hyenas.

5 See, e.g., Douglas (1967: 37; 1966: 101ff.).

6 See *Nuer Religion* (1956), whose index contains no entry under "skepticism," a term that figures prominently in the Zande book.

7 Arens does, of course, recognize the occurrence of "crisis cannibalism," when starvation drives people to eat human flesh.

8 Sahlins (1983: 88). See also Sanday 1986.

9 See, e.g., Best (1902).

10 This seems also to be the general conclusion reached by other Amazonian Indian specialists – e.g., Dr. S. Dreyfus-Gamelon, Dr. Joanna Overing, and Dr. Peter Rivière (personal communications.)

11 Joseph Tubiana reports (personal communication) that in Ethiopia to "give someone a village to eat" signifies granting the person concerned the right to tax (and live off) the village in question. Among the Zaghawa, Marie-José Tubiana has recorded, political usurpation may be represented as a process of seduction with the aid of tempting food.

12 See Jones (1949: 120).

13 See "Cannibal of the Bois de Boulogne," *The Observer*, June 21, 1981. This case has potentially wider symbolic reverberations; the gruesome incident has been made the subject of a best-selling novel by the Japanese playwright Juro Kara, which won a prestigious Japanese literary award in 1983. Some commentators have interpreted the book as displaying the vengeance of a small Oriental who feels he is the victim of white oppression.

6: THE SHAMAN'S CAREER

1 See, e.g., Hultkrantz (1973), Siikala (1978), and Siikala and Hoppal 1992.

2 For recent studies by contemporary Soviet scholars see Basilov (1981; 1984). For the work of Hungarian scholars see Voigt (1977), Dioszegi (1968), and Hoppal (1984).

3 See, e.g., Lommel (1965).

4 Here, however, in addition to the strong tradition of specialists working on Siberian and Mongolian shamanism (e.g., Lot-Falck, and more recently Hamayon), it is important to note the work of Leiris (1958; 1980). Although dealing only with Ethiopia, Leiris was one of the first to point to the importance of shamans and shamanism in Africa in general – a region explicitly omitted in Mircea Eliade's magisterial work, which though first published in 1951 and dedicated to the author's "French masters and colleagues," is left oddly unmentioned by Leiris.

5 See de Martino (1948). This point was made forcefully and elegantly in "Shamanism: history, limits and prospects for Research in Italy" (paper presented by Romano Mastromattei at the symposium, The Comparative Study of the Early Forms of Religion: Shamanism in Eurasia; Sarospatak, Hungary, September, 1981). With his notion of spirits as hypotheses, Shirokogoroff in my opinion also anticipates many of the ideas of the contemporary English anthropologist Robin Horton (1968). It would also not be an exaggeration to claim Shirokogoroff as a revolutionary pioneer of ethno-medicine. To see, as he did in 1935, that "European medicine itself is an ethnographical phenomenon" was truly remarkable. Nor is Shirokogoroff's influence limited to his publications. China's leading contemporary anthropologist, Professor Fei Xiao-Tong, was, he has told me, one of Shirokogoroff's students, and was sent by him to study anthropology with Malinowski at the London School of Economics.

6 For a recent discussion of the literature see Oosten (1980).

7 See, e.g., Codere (1966: 120–71).

8 In the case of the Swedish anthropologist Knutsson's (1967) brilliant analysis of Oromo religion, which is explicitly modeled on Lienhardt's Dinka study, this influence is so strong that the term *shaman* seems to have been completely exorcised, although the phenomenon is clearly present.

9 See Hitchcock and Jones (1976) and Crapanzano and Garrison (1977).

10 This Tungus origin is generally accepted. It has also been suggested that the word may ultimately derive from the Vedic *sram*, to heat oneself or practice austerities, and *sramana*, practitioner of austerities or ascetic. According to Sir Harold Bailey (quoted in Blacker 1975: 318) the word came to Asia from India in the Shan Kingdom form *samana*, reaching China as *shamen*, and Japan as *shamon*. See also Voigt (1977). The distinguished authority on Tungusic languages Robert Austerlitz, however, considers the hypothesis of an Indian origin of the Tungus form "moribund" (personal communication).

11 Eliade (1951: 434). All references here are to the 1951 French edition.

12 Notably Lommel (1965).

13 *Der Ursprung der Gottesidee* (1912–55: xii).

14 As Anna-Leena Siikala rightly stresses in her splendid assessment of the Siberian evidence (1978: 333), such stimulants are not, of course, by any means essential.

15 For more recent work on Tungus and Siberian shamanism, see (in addition to Siikala) Anisimov in Michael, ed. (1963); and others cited in Voigt (1977); Lot-Falck (1953, 1973); Bayle, ed. (1977); Basilov (1984); and Potapov (1978). On Buryat shamanism see Hamayon (1978: 17–45; 1981; 1990) and Humphrey (1979: 235–60). On Lapp shamanism see Bachman and Hultkrantz (1978).

16 Blacker (1975); see also Hori (1968).

17 As will be evident, this definition closely follows Shirokogoroff.

18 Eliade (1951), especially Chapter 4.

19 Siikala (1978: 335–6): "Since shamanic seances are for the most part precisely healing events, it is scarcely a coincidence that basically parallel spirit and demon possessions appear in the same regions. Thus the explanation for illness: 'the demon has penetrated the patient' would in turn add to the popularity of the possession type technique of shamanising."

20 Siikala (1978). Professor Siikala's role-taking model of shamanism refers primarily to the structure of the seance itself. Since, however, it is often observed with justice that in the seance the shaman recapitulates his original traumatic induction, one would expect to find a certain parallelism between the structure of the initiation process and that of the seance. Contrary to the interpretation placed on our processual schema of shamanic initiation by my friend Jean-Paul Olivier de Sardan (1994), it is not argued here that shamanism, possession, ecstasy, and sorcery are indistinguishable phenomena. Rather, my analysis seeks to explore their inter-relations.

21 For the Malaysian pattern see, e.g., Kessler (1977), and Laderman 1991.

22 See particularly Leiris ([1958] 1980: 103ff.).

23 Basilov (1981).

7: EXPELLING SPIRITS, CONTROLLING WOMEN

1 This was carried out while I was a British Academy Visiting Professor at the Universiti Sains Malaya. I am most grateful to both institutions for this opportunity and to my immediate host, Professor Wazir Jahan Karim and her colleagues. An earlier version of this paper was presented at a Round Table discussion at the Department of Social Sciences, at the Istituto Universitario Orientale, Naples, at Professor Vittorio Lanternari's seminar at the University of Rome, and at the Religions-ethnologie Symposium held at the University of Mainz in June

1989. I am very grateful for comments received on these occasions.

2 The *bomohs* with whom I discussed mental illness, tended to distinguish between "madness" (*gila*) caused by spirits, and "madness" caused either by brain damage or hereditary factors. The latter cases seem to be considered untreatable by *bomohs*.

3 I owe this information on Milingo to Diordana Scharuty, of the CNRS, who has been conducting research on the Archbishop's regular devotees in Rome. See also Lanternari 1988, for and Milingo in Africa, ter Haar and Ellis 1988.

4 Exorcism can even play a central role in a cult group's ritual, as Davis (1980) has elegantly demonstrated in the context of one of Japan's "new Religions."

5 A striking recent European instance of this is the suppression by the Vatican of Archbishop Milingo's exorcistic rituals in Rome.

8: THE POWER OF THE PAST: AFRICAN "SURVIVALS" IN ISLAM

1 Ferchiou (1972).

2 See, e.g., Gellner (1982).

3 See Arberry (1950: 23). In the context of Somali Islam this is discussed by Andrzejewski (1974).

4 Marx (1977: 29–50).

5 I. M. Lewis (1955: 56).

6 The main sources are discussed in Lewis (1971: 101–4).

7 Swantz (1970); see also Strobel (1979).

8 *The Influence of Islam on Africa* (London, Longman, 1968).

9 "Conversion reconsidered: some historical aspects of religious conversions in Black Africa," *Africa* 43 (1973).

10 See I. M. Lewis, ed. (1980a: vii, 59) and Horton (1975).

11 Parkin (1970; 1972).

12 Braukamper (1977); Andrzejewski (1975: 139–40). See also I. M. Lewis (1980b: 409–15).

13 In other contexts the word refers to immigrant groups or individuals attached to local Somali clans. It seems to have the general sense of something extraneous superimposed or grafted onto an object or person. The generic Somali term for "possession" is literally *gelid*, "entering."

14 Also known in Somali as "Ethiopian *sar*." The female cult leader is called *alaaqad*, probably derived from Amharic *alaqa*, priest. See also Giannattasio (1983).

15 Cf. I. M. Lewis (1971).

16 Compare Jon Anderson's interesting observation that in Muslim Afghanistan upwardly mobile women often adopt the veil while the "outwardly mobile" (i.e., nomadic) discard it (Anderson 1982: 397–420).

17 Luling (1991).

18 Saunders (1977); Morsy (1978; 1991). For a somewhat parallel situation in Kathmandu, see D. Gellner 1994.

19 In the Sudan, *zar* is also commonly referred to by the Arabic term *dastur*, "constitution" or "peg" – the latter word alluding to the hold the spirits exert on their human subjects. For recent accounts of Sudanese *zar*, see Samia al-Hadi al-Nagar (1980), Constantinides (1977), Anne Cloudsley (1983), and Ahmed Al-Shahi (1984: 28–44). See also Lewis *et al.* 1991.

20 Often ex-slaves, widows, or divorced women.

21 Personal communication, Professor Lidwien Kepteijns.

22 It is not implied that there is always a single cult for women and men. Frequently, as to some extent in Khartoum and on Maffia Island (Caplan 1975), there are separate cults for bourgeois wives and for low status men.

23 As, e.g., in the case of the Iranian cult of those "possessed of the atmosphere" (ahl-e-Haval) by *bad* (or "wind") spirits. See Marsden (1972).

24 Although several undated manuscripts chronicling events in sixteenth-century Ethiopia refer to *zar*, the first securely dated occurrence of the word appears to be a translation produced at the beginning of the nineteenth century by an old Ethiopian from Gondar, living in Cairo – see Rodinson (1964: 238–45), Plowden (1868: 264ff.), and Borelli (1890: 133). There is no specific reference to the *zar* cult in Lane's encyclopedic *Manners and Customs of the Modern Egyptians* (1836). In Khartoum, although the term *zar* is used, the spirits and their cult are perhaps more commonly referred to as *dastur* (cf. Arabic, "constitution"). It is thus intriguing that Lane (229ff.) should record in his day that citizens of Cairo regularly used this term to address the *jinns* that they thought filled the air. According to the late Professor Tijani al-Mahi, who conducted extensive historical and psychiatric research on the subject, *zar* came to the Sudan in 1905 and was recorded by Ali Pasha Mubarak in Egypt in the 1890s as a "calamity now spreading in our country." MacDonald (1911: 332) reports that *zar* was unknown in Egypt up to 1880. See also Natvig 1991.

25 Leiris (1980); Tubiana (1954: 76–90; 1991).

26 Leiris (1980: 38). Leiris (p. 58) also notes that in Gondar *zar* spirits temporarily disappeared after the death of Emperor Johannes in the Ethiopian defeat at the hands of the forces of the Sudanese Mahdi at the battle of Matamma in 1889.

27 See Chapter 3. Alpers (1981), "Female subculture in nineteenth century Zanzibar: the Kitimiri spirit possession cult" (unpublished manuscript), offers a similar interpretation of the expansion of this cult, which has Ethiopian connections, at a time of increasing Islamic orthodoxy.

28 See Westermarck (1926, vol. 1: 395–6). Crapanzano (1973), Eickelman (1981), and Jamous (1981).

29 This is, of course, equally true of the interplay between center and periphery in other world religions and ideologies, processes that in the Indian Hindu context have been well analyzed by Marriott (1955) in terms of "parochialization" (of the great tradition) and "universalization" (of the little tradition). For a valuable discussion of these issues in Islam, see Eickelman (1983: 1–16).

Bibliography

Abdalla, I. H. 1991. "Neither friend nor foe: the *malam* practitioner – *yan bori* relationship in Hausaland." In *Women's Medicine*, eds. I. M. Lewis *et al.* Edinburgh, Edinburgh University Press.

'Abdillah, M. F. and Andrzejewski, B. W. 1967. "The life of 'Ilmi Bownderi, a Somali poet who is said to have died of love." *J. Folkl. Inst.* 4, no. 2/3: 191–206.

Aberle, D. F. 1952. "Arctic hysteria and *latah* in Mongolia." *Trans. N.Y. Acad. Sci.*, ser. 2, no. 14: 291–7.

Ackerman, S. E. and Lee, R. L. M. 1981. "Communication and cognitive pluralism in a spirit possession event in Malaysia." *American Ethnologist*, 8: 789–99.

Agar, M. H. 1982. "Towards an ethnographic language." *American Anthropologist* 84, no. 4: 779–95.

Alexandre, P. 1974. "On some witches and a predicant." In *Choice and Change: Essays in Honour of Lucy Mair*, ed. J. Davis. London, Athlone Press.

al-Nagar, Samia al-Hadi. 1980. "Zaar practitioners and their assistants and followers in Omdurman." In *Urbanization and Urban Life in the Sudan*, in V. G. Pons, ed. University of Khartoum, Development Studies and Research Centre.

Alpers, E. A. 1981. "Female subculture in nineteenth century Zanzibar: the Kitimiri spirit possession cult." Unpublished ms. paper presented at conference on African Women in History, University of Santa Clara, May.

Al-Shahi, Ahmed. 1984. "Spirit possession and healing: the Zar among the Shaygiyya of the Northern Sudan." *Bulletin British Society for Middle Eastern Studies* 11, no. 1: 28–44.

Anderson, J. W. 1982. "Social interaction and the veil: comportment and the composition of interaction in Afghanistan." *Anthropos* 77: 397–420.

Andrzejewski, B. W. 1974. "The veneration of Sufi saints and its impact on the oral literature of the Somali people and on their literature in Arabic." *African Language Studies* 15: 15–53.

1975. "A genealogical note relevant to the dating of Sheikh Hussein of Bale." *Bulletin School of Oriental and African Studies* 38: 139–40.

Anisimov, A. F. 1963. "The shaman's tent of the Evenks and the origin of the shamanistic rite." In *Studies in Siberian Shamanism*, ed. H. N. Michael. Arctic Institute of North America, Anthropology of the North, Translations from Russian Sources, No. 4. Toronto, Toronto University Press.

Anonymous. 1972. *Department of Anthropology 1972–73* (pamphlet). London School of Economics and Political Science.

Arbery, A. J. 1950. *Sufism*. London, Allen & Unwin.

Ardener, E. 1972. "Belief and the problem of women." In *The Interpretation of Ritual*, ed. J. S. La Fontaine. London, Tavistock.

Ardener, E. and S. 1965. "A directory study of social anthropologists." *British Journal of Sociology* 16, no. 4: 295–314.

Arens, William. 1979. *The Man-Eating Myth: Anthropology and Anthropophagy*. London, Oxford University Press.

Atkinson, J. M. 1992. "Shamanism today." *Annual Review of Anthropology* 21: 307–30.

Bachman, L. and Hultkrantz, A. 1978. *Studies in Lapp Shamanism*. Stockholm, Almqvist and Wiksell.

Banton, M., ed. 1965. *The Relevance of Models for Social Anthropology*. London, Tavistock.

Barclay, H. B. 1964. *Buuri al Lamaab: A Suburban Village in the Sudan*. New York, Cornell University Press.

Basilov, V. N. 1981. 'Some results of the study of the vestiges of shamanism in Central Asia." International Congress of Anthropological and Ethnological Sciences, Intercongress, Holland.

1984. "The study of shamanism in Soviet ethnography." In *Shamanism in Eurasia*, ed. M. Hoppal. Gottingen, Herodot.

Bayle, D., ed. 1977. *Voyages Chamaniques: L'Ethnographie* (n.s.). Nos. 74–5.

Beattie, J. 1961. "Group aspects of Nyoro spirit mediumship cult." *Human Problems in British Central Africa (Rhodes-Livingstone Institute Journal)* 30: 11–38.

1963. "Witchcraft and sorcery in Bunyoro." In *Witchcraft and Sorcery in East Africa*, eds. J. Middleton and E. H. Winter. London, Routledge & Kegan Paul.

1966. "Ritual and social change." *Man* 1 (n.s.): 60–74.

1969. "Spirit mediumship in Bunyoro." In *Spirit Mediumship and Society in Africa*, eds. J. Beattie and J. Middleton. London, Routledge & Kegan Paul.

Beattie, J. and Middleton, J., eds. 1969. *Spirit Mediumship and Society in Africa*. London, Routledge & Kegan Paul.

Berger, I. 1976. "Rebels or status seekers? Women as spirit mediums." In *Women in Africa*, eds. N. J. Hafkin and E. G. Bay. Stanford, Stanford University Press.

Besmer, F. E. 1983. *Horses, musicians and gods: the Hausa cult of possession trance*. Massachusetts, Bergin and Garvey.

Best, Elsdon. 1902. "Notes on the art of war as conducted by the Maori of New Zealand." *Journal of the Polynesian Society* 11, nos. 41–4.

Biebuyck, D. 1953. "Repartitions et droits du pangolin chez les Balega." *Zaire* 7: 899–924.

Bjerke, S. 1981. *Religion and Misfortune: The Bacwezi Complex and the other Spirit Cults of the Zinza of Northwestern Tanzania*. Oslo, Universitetsforlaget.

Blacker, C. 1975. *The Catalpa Bow*. London, Allen and Unwin.

Bloch, M. and Parry, J., eds. 1972. *Death and the Regeneration of Life*. Cambridge, Cambridge University Press.

Bohannan, P. 1957. *Justice and Judgement among the Tiv*. London, Oxford University Press.

Bohannan, P. and Dalton, G., eds. 1962. *Markets in Africa*. Evanston, Ill.: Northwestern University Press.

Borelli, J. 1890. *Ethiopie Meridionale*. Paris, Ancienne Maison Quantin.

Bourguignon, E. 1976. *Possession*. San Francisco, Chandler & Sharp.

Bouteiller, M. 1950. *Chamanisme et guerison magique*. Paris, Presses Universitaires de France.

Braukamper, U. 1977. "Islamic principalities in south-east Ethiopia between the 13th and 16th centuries." *Ethiopianist Notes* 1, no. 1: 17–56; *Ethiopianist Notes* 1, no. 2: 1–43.

Brown, P. and Tuzin, D., eds. 1983. *The Ethnography of Cannibalism*. Washington, D.C., Society for Psychological Anthropology.

Bulmer, R. 1967. "Why is the cassowary not a bird? A problem of zoological taxonomy among the Karam of the New Guinea Highlands." *Man* (n.s.) 2: 5–25.

Buxton, J. C. 1973. *Religion and Healing in Mandari*. Oxford, Clarendon Press.

Caplan, A. P. 1975. *Choice and Constraint in a Swahili Community*. London, Oxford University Press.

Casagrande, J. B., ed. 1960. *In the Company of Man*. New York, Harper.

Casagrande, J. B. and Gladwin, T. eds. 1956. *Some Uses of Anthropology: Theoretical and Applied*. Washington, D.C., Anthropological Society.

Castiglione, M. 1977. "Il tarantismo oggi: proposte per una verifica." *Crit. sociol.* 11: 43–69.

Cerulli, E. 1923. "Note sul movimento musulmano della Somalia." *Riv. Stud. Orient* 10: 1–36.

Chavunduka, G. 1980. "Witchcraft and the law." (Inaugural lecture delivered at the University of Zimbabwe.) *Zambezia* 8: 129–47.

Clifford, J. 1983. "Power and dialogue in ethnography: Marcel Griaule's initiation." In *Observers Observed*, ed. G. W. Stocking. Madison, University of Wisconsin Press.

Clifford, J. and Marcus G., eds. 1986. *Writing Culture*. Berkeley, University of California Press.

Cloudsley, Anne. 1983. *Women of Omdurman: Life, Love and the Cult of Virginity*. London, Ethnographica.

Codere, H., ed. 1966. *Franz Boas: Kwakiutl Ethnography*. Chicago, University of Chicago Press.

Colajanni, A. 1982. "Shamanism and social change: the killing of an Achuar shaman. Facts and interpretations." Manuscript paper, 44th Congress of Americanists, Manchester.

Colson, E. 1958. *Marriage and the Family among the Platau Tonga of Northern Rhodesia*. Manchester, Manchester University Press.

1969. "Spirit possession among the Tonga of Zambia." In *Spirit Mediumship and Society in Africa*, eds. J. Beattie and J. Middleton. London, Routledge & Kegan Paul.

Constantinedes, P. 1977. "Ill at ease and sick at heart: symbolic behaviour in a Sudanese healing cult." In *Symbols and Sentiments*, ed. I. M. Lewis. London, Academic Press.

Crapanzano, V. 1973. *The Hamadsha: A Study in Moroccan Ethnopsychiatry*. Berkeley, University of California Press.

1992. *Hermes' Dilemma and Hamlet's Revenge: On the Epistemology of Interpretation*. Cambridge, Mass., Harvard University Press.

Crapanzano, V. and Garrison, V., eds. 1977. *Case Studies in Spirit Possession*. London, Wiley.

Crawford, J. R. 1967. *Witchcraft and Sorcery in Rhodesia*. London, Oxford University Press.

Czaplicka, M. A. 1949. *Aboriginal Siberia*. Oxford, Clarendon Press.

Davis, J., ed. 1974. *Choice and Change: Essays in Honour of Lucy Mair*. London, Athlone Press.

Davis, W. 1980. *Dojo: Magic and Exorcism in Modern Japan*. Stanford, Stanford University Press.

de Heusch, Luc. 1962. "Cultes de possession et religions initiatiques de salut en Afrique." *Annales du Centre d'Etudes des Religions*, vol. 2. Brussels, Institut de sociologie de l'université libre de Bruxelles.

1964. "Structure et praxis sociales chez les Lele du Kasai." *L'Homme* 4: 87–109.

1966. *Le Ruanda et la civilisation interlacustre*. Bruxelles, Institut de Sociologie de l'Université Libre.

1971. *Pourquoi l'epouser?* Paris, Gallimard.

1985. *Sacrifice in Africa*. Bloomington, Indiana University Press.

1991. "On Griaule on trial." *Current Anthropology* 33: 434–7.

1993. "Hunting the pangolin." *Man* 28, no. 1: 159–61.

de Martino, E. 1948. *Il Mondo Magico*. Turin, Einaudi.

de Martino, E. 1961. *La terra del rimorso*. Milan, Il Saggiatore.

de Sardan, O. J.-P. 1994. "Possession, affliction et folie: les ruses de la thérapisation." *L'Homme* 13, xxiv (3): 7–27.

Delaby, L. 1977. *Chamanes Toungouses*. Nanterre, Université de Paris, Laboratoire d'Ethnologie et de Sociologie Comparative, Centre d'Etudes Mongoles.

Dermenghem, E. 1954. *Le Culte des saints dans l'Islam Maghrebin*. Paris, Gallimard.

Devereux, G. 1956. "Normal and abnormal: the key problem of psychiatric anthropology." In *Some Uses of Anthropology*, eds. J. B. Casagrande and T. Gladwin. Washington, D.C., Anthropological Society.

1961. *Mohave Ethnopsychiatry and Suicide: the Psychiatric Knowledge and the Psychic Disturbances of an Indian Tribe*. Washington, D.C., Smithsonian Institution Bureau of American Ethnology, bulletin 175.

Dioszegi, V. 1968. *Tracing Shamans in Siberia*. Oosterhout, Anthropological Publications.

Douglas, M. 1954. "The Lele of the Kasai." In *African Worlds*, ed. D. Forde. London, Oxford University Press.

1957. "Animals in Lele religious symbolism." *Africa* 27: 46–58.

1963. *The Lele of Kasai*. London, Oxford University Press.

1966. *Purity and Danger*. London, Routledge & Kegan Paul.

1967. "Witch beliefs in central Africa." *Africa* 37, no. 1: 72–80.

1970. *Natural Symbols: Explorations in Cosmology*. London, Barrie & Rockliff.

1975. *Implicit Meanings*. London, Routledge.

1990. "The pangolin revisited: a new approach to animal symbolism." In *Signifying Animals: Human Meaning in the Natural World*, ed. R. Willis. London, Hyman.

1993. "Hunting the Pangolin." *Man* 28, no. 1: 161–4.

Douglas, M., ed. 1970. *Witchcraft Confessions and Accusations*. London, Tavistock.

Douglas, M. and Kaberry, P., eds. 1969. *Man in Africa*. London, Tavistock.

Dubb, A., ed. 1960. *Myth in Modern Africa: The Fourteenth Conference Proceedings of the Rhodes-Livingstone Institute for Social Research*. Lusaka, Rhodes Livingstone Institute.

Earthy, E. 1933. *Valenge Women*. London, Oxford University Press.

Echard, N. 1978. "La pratique religieuse des femmes dans une société d'hommes: les Hausa du Niger." *Revue française de sociologie* 19: 551–62.

Edel, M. M. 1957. *The Chiga of Western Uganda*. London, Oxford University Press.

Eickelman, D. F. 1981. *The Middle East*. New Jersey, Prentice-Hall.

1983. "The study of Islam in local contexts." *Contributions to Asian Studies* 18: 1–16.

Eliade, Mircea. 1951. *Le chamanisme et les techniques archaiques de l'extase*. Paris, Librairie Payot.

Ellen, R. F. 1972. "The marsupial in Nuaulu ritual behaviour." *Man* (n.s.) 7: 223–38.

Ellen, R. F., ed. 1984. *Ethnographic Research: A Guide to General Conduct*. London, Academic Press.

Elliot, A. J. A. 1955. *Chinese Spirit Medium Cults in Singapore*. London, Athlone Press.

Endicott, K. M. 1970. *An Analysis of Malay Magic*. Oxford: Oxford University Press.

Epstein, A. L. 1958. *Politics in an Urban African Community*. Manchester, Manchester University Press.

1979. "Unconscious factors in the response to social crisis: a case study from central Africa." In *The Psychoanalytic Study of Society*, vol. 8. New Haven, Yale University Press.

Evans-Pritchard, E. E. 1937. *Witchcraft, Oracles and Magic among the Azande*. Oxford, Clarendon Press.

1951. *Social Anthropology*. London, Cohen & West.

1956. *Nuer Religion*. Oxford, Clarendon Press.

1965. *Theories of Primitive Religion*. Oxford, Clarendon Press.

1965. "Zande cannibalism." In *The Position of Women in Primitive Societies and Other Essays in Social Anthropology*. London, Faber.

1966. "Twins, birds and vegetables" (letter). *Man* 1, no. 3: 398–9.

Fardon, R. 1990. *Localizing Strategies: Regional Traditions of Ethnographic Writing*. Edinburgh, Scottish Academic Press.

1993. "Spiders, pangolins and zoo visitors." *Man* 28, no. 2: 361–3.

Ferchiou, Sophie. 1972. "Survivances mystiques et cultes de possession dans le maraboutisme Tunisien." *L'Homme* 12, no. 3: 47–69.

    1991. "The possession cults of Tunisia." In *Women's Medicine: the Zar-Bori cult in Africa and beyond*, eds. I. M. Lewis, A. as-Safi and S. Hurreiz. Edinburgh, Edinburgh University Press.

Field, M. J. 1960. *Search for Security: An Ethno-psychiatric Study of Rural Ghana*. London, Faber.

Firth, Raymond. 1959. "Problem and assumption in an anthropological study of religion." *Journal of the Royal Anthropological Institute* 89: 129–40.

    1960. "A Polynesian aristocrat (Tikopia)." In *In the Company of Man*, ed. J. B. Casagrande. New York, Harper.

    1966. "Twins, birds and vegetables: problems of identification in primitive religious thought." *Man* 1 (n.s.): 1–17.

    1967a. *Tikopia Ritual and Belief*. London, George Allen & Unwin.

    1967b. "Ritual and drama in Malay spirit mediumship." *Comparative Studies in Society and History* 9: 190–207.

Firth, Rosemary. 1972. "From wife to anthropologist." In *Crossing Cultural Boundaries*, eds. S. T. Kimball and J. B. Watson. San Francisco, Chandler.

Fisher, H. J. 1973. "Conversion reconsidered: some historical aspects of religious conversions in Black Africa." *Africa* 43: 27–40.

Forge, A. 1970. "Prestige, influence and sorcery: a New Guinea example." In *Witchcraft Confessions and Accusations*, ed. M. Douglas. London, Tavistock.

    1972. "The Golden Fleece." *Man* 7, no. 4: 527–40.

Forsyth, D. 1983. "The beginnings of Brazilian anthropology: Jesuits and Tupinamba cannibalism." *Journal of Anthropological Research* 2: 147–78.

Fortes, M. 1959. *Oedipus and Job in West African Religion*. Cambridge, Cambridge University Press.

Fortes, M. and Dieterlen, G., eds. 1965. *African Systems of Thought*. London, Oxford University Press.

Fortune, R. 1953. *Manus Religion*. Philadelphia, American Philosophical Society.

Foster, G. 1965. "Peasant society and the image of limited good." *American Anthropologist* 67: 293–315.

Fraenkel, P. J. 1959. *Wayaleshi*. London, Weidenfeld & Nicolson.

Freilich, M., ed. 1970. *Marginal Natives: Anthropologists at Work*. New York, Harper.

Freud, S. [1913] 1950. *Totem and Taboo*. London, Routledge & Kegan Paul.

Friedland, W. H. 1960. "Some urban myths in East Africa." In *Myth in Modern Africa*, ed. A. Dubb. Lusaka, Rhodes Livingstone Institute.

Gallini, C. 1967. *I rituali dell'Argia*. Padua, CEDAM.

1988. *La ballerina variopinta: una festa di Guarigione in Sardegna*. Naples, Ligouri.

Geertz, C. 1984. "Distinguished lecture: anti anti-relativism." *American Anthropologist* 86, no. 2: 263–78.

Gellner, D. N. 1994. "Priests, healers, mediums and witches: the context of possession in the Kathmandu valley, Nepal." *Man* 29 no. 1: 27–48.

Gellner, E. 1962. "Concepts and society." *Proceedings Fifth World Congress of Sociologists*, 1.

1982. *Muslim Society*. Cambridge, Cambridge University Press.

1992. *Postmodernism, Reason, and Religion*. New York, Routledge.

Geschiere, P. and Fisiy, C. 1994. "Domesticating personal violence: witchcraft, courts and confessions in Cameroon." *Africa* 64, no. 3: 323–41.

Giannattasio, F. 1983. "Somalia: La terapia Corentico-musicale del Mingis." *Culture musicale, quaderni di etnomusicologia* 2, no. 3: 93–119.

Gifford, E. W. 1929. *Tongan Society*. Honolulu, Bernice P. Bishop Museum.

Gluckman, M. 1954. *Rituals of Rebellion in South-East Africa*. Manchester, Manchester University Press.

1963. *Order and Rebellion in Tribal Africa*. London, Cohen & West.

Gombrich, R. and Obeysekere, G. 1988. *Buddhism Transformed: Religious Change in Sri Lanka*. New Jersey, Princeton University Press.

Greenberg, J. 1946. *The Influence of Islam on a Sudanese Religion*. New York, American Ethnological Society.

Griaule, M. 1965. *Conversations with Ogotommeli*. London, Oxford University Press.

Gussow, Z. 1960. "*Pibloktoq* (hysteria) among the polar Eskimo." *Psychoanalysis and the Social Sciences*. ed. W. Muensterberger. New York, International University Press.

Hadfield, J. A. 1969. *Dreams and Nightmares*. Harmondsworth, Penguin.

Hafkin, N. J. and Bay, E. G., eds. 1976. *Women in Africa*. Stanford, University Press.

Hall, T. H. 1962. *The Spiritualists*. London, Duckworth.

Hallpike, C. R. 1972. *The Konso of Ethiopia*. Oxford, Clarendon Press.

Haltenorth, T. and Diller, H. 1980. *A Field Guide to the Mammals of Africa*. London, Collins.

Hamayon, R. 1978. "Le heros de service." *L'Homme* 18, no. 3/4: 17–45.
1984. "Is there a typically female exercise of shamanism in patrilinear societies such as the Buryat?" In *Shamanism in Eurasia*, ed. M. Hoppal. Göttingen, Herodot.
1990. *La chasse à l'âme: esquisse d'une théorie du chamanisme siberien*. Nanterre, Société d'ethnologie.

Hammond-Tooke, W. D. 1981. *Boundaries and Belief: The Structure of a Sotho Worldview*. Johannesburg, Witwatersrand University Press.

Harrington, C. and Whiting, J. M. 1972. "Socialisation process and personality." In *Psychological Anthropology*, ed. F. L. K. Hsu. Cambridge, Mass., Schenkman.

Harris, G. 1957. "Possession 'hysteria' in a Kenyan tribe." *American Anthropologist* 59: 1046–66.

Harris, M. 1977. *Cannibals and Kings*. New York, Random House.

Harwood, A. 1970. *Witchcraft, Socery and Social Categories among the Safwa*. London, Oxford University Press.

Hitchcock, J. T. and Jones, R. L., eds. 1976. *Spirit Possession in the Nepal Himalayas*. Warminster, Arris and Phillips.

Hjort, A. 1979. *Savanna Town: Rural Ties and Urban Opportunities in Northern Kenya*. Stockholm University, Studies in Social Anthropology.

Hogbin, H. I. 1934. *Law and Order in Polynesia*. London, Christophers.

Hollingshead, A. B. and Redlich, F. C. 1958. *Social Class and Mental Illness*. New York, John Wiley.

Holm, N. G., ed. 1982. *Religious Ecstasy*. Stockholm, Alonquist and Wiksell.

Hoppal, M. 1984. "Traces of shamanism in Hungarian folk beliefs." In *Shamanism in Eurasia*, ed. M. Hoppal. Göttingen, Herodot, pp. 430–49.

Hori, I. 1968. *Folk Religion in Japan*. Chicago, University of Chicago Press.

Horton, R. 1961. "Destiny and the unconscious in west Africa." *Africa* 31: 110–16.
1968. "Neo-Tyloreanism: sound sense or sinister prejudice." *Man* 3, no. 4: 625–34.
1975. "On the rationality of conversion." *Africa* 45: 373–99.

Hsu, F. L. K., ed. 1961. *Psychological Anthropology: Approaches to Culture and Personality*. Homewood, Ill., Dorsey Press. [See also second revised edition, 1972, *Psychological Anthropology*. Cambridge, Mass., Schenkman.]

Hugh-Jones, S. 1980. *The Palm and the Pleiades*. Cambridge, Cambridge University Press.

Hultkrantz, A. 1973. "A definition of shamanism." *Temenos* 9: 25–37.

Humphrey, C. 1979. "The uses of genealogy: a historical study of the nomadic and sedentarised Buryat." In *Pastoral Production and Society*. Cambridge, Cambridge University Press.

Hunn, E. 1979. "The abominations of Leviticus revisited." In *Classifications in Their Social Contexts*, eds. R. F. Ellen and D. Reason. London, Academic Press.

Hunter, M. 1936. *Reaction to Conquest*. London, Oxford University Press.

Hurgonje, S. 1931. *Mekka in the Later Part of the Nineteenth Century*, trans. J. H. Monahan. Leiden, E. J. Brill.

Huxley, A. 1952. *The Devils of Loudon*. London, Chatto & Windus.

Ivens, W. G. 1927. *Melanesians of the S.E. Solomon Islands*. London, Kegan Paul.

Jahoda, G. 1970a. "A psychologist's perspective." In *Socialisation: The Approach from Social Anthropology*, ed. P. Mayer. (A.S.A. monograph no. 8.) London, Tavistock.

1970b. "Supernatural beliefs and changing cognitive structures among Ghanaian university students." *Journal of Cross-Cultural Psychology* 115–30.

1971. "Social-psychological reflections on religious changes in Ghana." *Religion*: 24–31.

Jamous, R. 1981. *Honneur et Baraka, les structures traditionelles dans le Rif*. Cambridge, Cambridge University Press.

Jarvie, I. C. 1983. "The problem of the ethnographic real." *Current Anthropology* 24: 313–26.

Jennings, S. 1995. *Theatre, Ritual and Transformation: The Senoi Temiars*. London, Routledge.

Jones, Ernest. 1949. *On the Nightmare*. London, Hogarth Press.

Junod, H. A. 1922. *The Life of a South African Tribe*. New York, University Books.

Kaberry, P. M. 1969. "Witchcraft of the sun: incest in Nso." In *Man in Africa*, eds. M. Douglas and P. Kaberry. London, Tavistock.

Kapferer, B. 1983. *A Celebration of Demons*. Bloomington, Indiana University Press.

Karim, Wazir-Jahan. 1981. *Ma' Betsiek Concepts of Living Things*. London, Athlone Press.

1984. "Malay midwives and witches." *Social Science and Medicine* 18, no. 2: 159–66.

1992. *Women and Culture: Between Malay Adat and Islam*. Boulder, Westview Press.

Karim, Wazir-Jahan, ed. 1990. *Emotions of Culture: A Malay Perspective*. Singapore, Oxford University Press.

Karp, I. and Bird, C. S., eds. 1980. *Explorations in African Systems of Thought*. Bloomington, Indiana University Press.

Kessler, C. S. 1977. "Conflict and sovereignty in Kelantanese Malay spirit seances." In *Case Studies in Possession*, eds. V. Crapanzano and V. Garrison. New York, Wiley.

Kiev, A., ed. 1964. *Magic, Faith and Healing*. New York, Free Press of Glencoe.

1972. *Transcultural Psychiatry*. New York, The Free Press.

Kimball, S. T. and Watson, J. B., eds. 1972. *Crossing Cultural Boundaries*. San Francisco, Chandler.

Kluckhohn, C. 1944. *Navaho Witchcraft*. Cambridge, Mass., Peabody Museum.

Knutsson, K. E. 1967. *Authority and Change*. Goteborg, Etnografiska Museet.

Koritschoner, H. 1936. "Ngoma Ya Sheitani: an east African native treatment for psychical disorder." *Journal of the Royal Anthropological Institute* 66: 209–17.

Kremser, M. 1981. "Das bild der 'menschenfressenden Niam-Niam'." In Den Berichten Deutscher Forschengsreisender des 19 Jahrhunderts. *Wiener Ethnohistorische Blatter*, 21.

Krige, E. J. 1936. *The Social System of the Zulus*. London, Longmans.

Kriss, R. and Kriss-Heinrich, M. 1962. *Volksglaube in Bereichdes Islam*. Wiesbaden, Otto Harrassowitz.

Kuper, A. 1994. "Culture, identity and the project of a cosmopolitan anthropology." *Man* 29, no. 3: 537–54.

La Fontaine, J. S., ed. 1972. *The Interpretation of Ritual*. London, Tavistock.

Laderman, C. 1987. "Main Peteri: synopses of Three Shamanistic performances." *J. Malay Branch, Royal Asiatic Society* 60, Part 2.

1991. *Taming the Wind of Desire: Psychology, Medicine, and Aesthetics in Malay Shamanistic Performances*. Berkeley, University of California Press.

Lane, E. W. [1836] 1954. *Manners and Customs of the Modern Egyptians*. London, Everyman.

Lanternari, V. 1963. *The Religions of the Oppressed*. London, Macgibbon & Kee.

1988. "L'Africa cattolica a Roma: il culto terapeutico di Emmanuel Miligno." *Metaxu* 6: 65–81.

Larose, S. 1977. "The meaning of Africa in Haitian vodu." In *Symbols and Sentiments*, ed. I. M. Lewis. London, Academic Press.

Last, M. 1976. "The presentation of sickness in a community of non-Muslim Hausa." In *Social Anthropology and Medicine*, ed. J. B. Lodon. London, Academic Press.

1979. "Some economic aspects of conversion in Hausaland (Nigeria)." *Conversion to Islam*, ed. N. Levtzion. New York, Holmes & Meier.

Laubscher, B. J. F. 1937. *Sex, Custom and Psychopathology*. London, Routledge.

Leach, E. R. 1961. *Rethinking Anthropology*. London, Athlone.

1966. "Virgin birth" (the Henry Myers Lecture). *Proceedings of the Royal Anthropological Institute for 1966*: 39–49.

1970. *Lévi-Strauss*. London, Fontana.

Lee, S. G. 1950. "Some Zulu concepts of psychogenic disorder." *S. Afr. J. Soc. Res.* 2: 9–16.

1969. "Spirit possession among the Zulu." In *Spirit Mediumship and Society in Africa*, eds. J. Beattie and J. Middleton. London, Routledge & Kegan Paul.

Legué, G. 1880. *Urbain Grandier et les possédés de Loudon*. Paris, Baschet.

Leiris, M. 1938. "La croyance aux genies 'Zar' en Ethiopie du Nord." *Journal de la psychologie normale et pathologique* 25, no. 1/2: 107–25.

1958. *La possession et ses aspects theatraux chez les Ethiopiens de Gondar*. Paris, Plon. [See also second edition, 1980. Paris, Sycomore.]

Lessa, W. A. and Vogt, E. Z., eds. 1958. *Reader in Comparative Religion*. New York, Row, Peterson.

Levine, D. N. 1965. *Wax and Gold: Tradition and Innovation in Ethiopian Culture*. Chicago, University of Chicago Press.

Levine, R. 1963. "Witchcraft and sorcery in a Gusii community." In *Witchcraft and Sorcery in East Africa*, eds. J. Middleton and E. H. Winter. London, Routledge & Kegan Paul.

Lévi-Strauss, C. 1966. *Mythologiques II: du miel aux cendres*. Paris, Plon.

1970. *The Raw and the Cooked*. London: Jonathan Cape. [English translation of *Mythologiques I: le cru et le cuit*. Paris, Plon, 1964.]

1971. *Mythologiques IV: l'homme nu*. Paris, Plon.

[1963] 1977. *Structural Anthropology*. Harmondsworth, Penguin Books.

Lewis, G. 1975. *Knowledge of Illness in a Sepik Society*. London, Athlone Press.

Lewis, I. M. 1955, 1956. "Sufism in Somaliland." *Bulletin, School of Oriental and African Studies* 17, no. 3: 581–602; 18, no. 1: 146–60.

1965. "Problems in the comparative study of unilineal descent." In *The Relevance of Models for Social Anthropology*, ed. M. Banton. London, Tavistock.

1966. "Spirit possession and deprivation cults." *Man* 1 (n.s.): 307–29.

1967. "Spirits and the sex war." *Man* 2, no. 4: 626–8.

1969. "Spirit possession in northern Somaliland." In *Spirit Mediumship and Society in Africa*, eds. J. Beattie and J. Middleton. London, Routledge & Kegan Paul.

1971. *Ecstatic Religion*. Harmondsworth, Penguin Books.

1976. *Social Anthropology in Perspective*. Harmondsworth, Penguin Books. (Revised edition, Cambridge University Press, 1985.)

1977. "Introduction." In *Symbols and Sentiments*, ed. I. M. Lewis. London, Academic Press.

1980a. "Introduction." In *Islam in Tropical Africa*. London, Hutchinson. [Original publication 1966, Oxford University Press.]

1980b. "The Western Somali Liberation Front (WSLF) and the legacy of Sheikh Hussein of Bale." In *Modern Ethiopia*, ed. J. Tubiana. Rotterdam, Balkema.

1983. "Spirit possession and biological reductionism: a rejoinder to Kehoe and Giletti." *American Anthropologist* 85, no. 2: 412–13, 416–17.

1989. *Ecstatic Religion: A Study of Shamanism and Spirit Possession* (second edition). London, Routledge. (Original publication, 1971, Penguin Books.)

1993a. "Hunting the pangolin." *Man* 28, no. 1: 165–6.

1993b. "Spiders, pangolins and zoo visitors." *Man* 28, no. 2: 363.

Lewis, I. M., Hurreiz, S. and as-Safi, A., eds. 1991. *Women's Medicine: The Zar-Bori Cult in Africa and Beyond*. Edinburgh, Edinburgh University Press.

Lieban, R. 1967. *Cebuana Sorcery*. Berkeley, University of California Press.

Lienhardt, G. 1961. *Divinity and Experience: The Religion of the Dinka*. Oxford, Clarendon Press.

Lindblom, G. 1920. *The Akamba in British East Africa*. Uppsala, Appelbergs Boktrykeri Abtieblolag.

Linton, R. 1933. *The Tantala: A Hill Tribe of Madagascar*. Chicago, Field Museum of Natural History.

Little, A. 1965. "An 'expectancy' estimate of hospitalisation rates for mental illness.' *British Journal of Sociology* 16: 221–31.

Littlejohn, James. 1970. "Twins, birds etc." *Bijdragen Tot de Taal-, Land- en Volkenkunde* 126, no. 1: 91–114.

Lommel, A. 1965. *Die Weltder fruhen Jager, Modizianmaner, Schamamen, Kunstler*. Munich, Staatlicher Museum fur Volkerkunde.

Lot-Falck, E. 1953. *Les rites de chasse chez des peuples siberiens*. Paris, Gallimard.

  1973. "Le chamanisme en Siberie: essai de mise au point." *Asie du Sud-Est et Monde Insulindien* 4, no. 3: 1–10.

  1977. "A propos du terme chamane." *Etudes mongols et siberiennes* 8. Nanterre.

Loudon, J. B. 1959. "Psychogenic disorders and social conflict among the Zulu." In *Culture and Mental Health*, ed. M. K. Opler. New York, Macmillan.

Lowie, R. 1920. *Primitive Society*. London, Routledge.

Luling, V. 1991. "Some possession cults in southern Somalia." In *Women's Medicine*, eds. I. M. Lewis *et al*. Edinburgh, Edinburgh University Press.

Maalouf, A. 1984. *The Crusades through Arab Eyes*. London, Al-Saqi Books.

MacCormack, C. 1980. "Proto-social to adult: a Sherbo transformation." In *Nature, Culture and Gender*, eds. C. MacCormack and M. Strathern. Cambridge, Cambridge University Press.

  1983. "Human leopards and crocodiles." In *The Ethnography of Cannibalism*, eds. P. Brown and D. Tuzin. Washington, D.C., Society for Psychological Anthropology.

MacDonald, B. 1911. *Aspects of Islam*. New York, Macmillan.

Macfarlane, A. 1970. *Witchcraft in Tudor and Stuart England*. London, Routledge.

MacGaffey, W. 1970. "The religious commissions of the Bakongo." *Man* 5: 27–30.

  1972. "Comparative analysis of central African religions." *Africa* 42: 21–31.

  1980. "African religions: types and generalisations." In *Explorations in African Systems of Thought*, eds. I. Karp and C. S. Bird. Bloomington, Indiana University Press.

Mahieu, W. de. 1980. *Structures et symboles*. Louvain, International African Institute.

  1985. *Qui a obstrué la cascade? Analyse sémantique du rituel de la circoncision chez les Komo du Zaïre*. Cambridge, Cambridge University Press.

Mair, Lucy. 1969. *Witchcraft*. London, Weidenfeld & Nicolson.

Malinowski, B. 1922. *Argonauts of the Western Pacific*. London, Routledge & Kegan Paul.

  1929. *The Sexual Life of Savages*. London, Routledge & Kegan Paul.

Marcus, G. and Fischer, M. 1986. *Anthropology as Cultural Critique*. Chicago, University of Chicago Press.

Marriott, McKim. 1955. "Little communities in an indigenous civilisation." In *Village India: Studies in the Little Community*, ed. McKim Marriott. Chicago, University of Chicago Press.

Marsden, D. J. 1972. "Spirit possession on the Persian Gulf." *Dyn* (Journal of the Durham Anthropological Society) 2.

Marwick, M. 1952. "The social context of Cewa witch beliefs." *Africa* 22: 120–35, 215–53.

1965. "Some problems in the sociology of sorcery and witchcraft." In *African Systems of Thought*, eds. M. Fortes and G. Dieterlen. London, Oxford University Press.

1970. "Witchcraft as a social strain-gauge." In *Witchcraft and Sorcery*, ed. M. Marwick. London, Penguin.

Marx, E. 1972. "Communal and individual pilgrimage: the region of saints' tombs in South Sinai." In *Regional Cults*, ed. R. P. Werbner. London, Academic Press.

Mastromattei, R. 1984. "History, limits and prospects for research on shamanism in Italy." In *Shamanism in Eurasia*, ed. M. Hoppal. Göttingen, Edition Herodot.

Mayer, P., ed. 1970. *Socialisation: The Approach from Social Anthropology*. (A.S.A. monograph no. 8.) London, Tavistock.

Mead, M. 1972. "Fieldwork in high cultures." In *Crossing Cultural Boundaries*, eds. S. T. Kimball and J. B. Watson. San Francisco, Chandler.

Mendelson, E. M. 1961. "A Messianic Buddhist Association in Upper Burma." *Bulletin of the School of Oriental and African Studies*, 24: 560–80.

Messing, S. D. 1958. "Group therapy and social status in the Zar cult of Ethiopia." *American Anthropologist* 60: 1120–7. [Reprinted in *Culture and Mental Health*, ed. M. K. Opler, New York, Macmillan.]

Metraux, A. 1959. *Voodoo in Haiti*. London, André Deutsch.

Michael, H. N., ed. 1963. *Studies in Siberian Shamanism*. (Arctic Institute of North America, Anthropology of the North, Translations from Russian Sources, no. 4.) Toronto, Toronto University Press.

Middleton, J. 1960. *Lugbara Religion*. London, Oxford University Press.

1969. "Oracles and divination among the Lugbara." In *Man in Africa*, eds. M. Douglas and P. Kaberry. London, Tavistock.

Middleton, J. and Winter, E., eds. 1963. *Witchcraft and Sorcery in East Africa*. London, Routledge & Kegan Paul.

Monfouga-Nicolas, J. 1972. *Ambivalence et culte de possession*. Paris, Editions Anthropos.

Montinaro, B. 1976. *Salento povero*. Ravenna.

Morsy, S. 1978. "Sex roles, power and illness in an Egyptian village." *American Ethnologist* 5, no. 1: 137–50.

Morton, A. 1973. "The changing position of Ethiopian women." Unpublished Social Science Research Council report, London.

 1977. "Dawit: competition and integration in an Ethiopian Wuqabi Cult Group." In *Case Studies in Spirit Possession*, eds. V. Crapanzano and V. Garrison. London, John Wiley.

Muensterberger, W., ed. 1960. *Psychoanalysis and the Social Sciences*. New York, International University Press.

Murphy, R. 1972. *The Dialectics of Social Life*. London, Allen and Unwin.

Nadel, S. F. 1946. "A study of Shamanism in the Nuba hills." *Journal of the Royal Anthropological Institute* 76: 25–37.

 1952. "Witchcraft in four African societies: an essay in comparison." *American Anthropologist* 54: 18–29.

Natvig, R. 1991. "Some notes on the history of the *Zar* cult in Egypt." In *Women's Medicine*, eds. I. M. Lewis *et al*. Edinburgh, Edinburgh University Press.

Needham, R. 1967. "Right and left in Banyoro symbolic classification." *Africa* 37, no. 4: 425–52.

 1972. *Belief, Language and Experience*. Oxford, Basil Blackwell.

 1976. Review of M. Douglas, *Implicit meanings: essays in anthropology*. *Man* (n.s.) 11: 127–8.

Nicolas, G. 1975. *Dynamique sociale et apprehension du monde au sein d'une société Hausa*. Paris, Musée de l'homme.

Ogot, Grace. 1988. *Land Without Thunder*. Nairobi, East Africa Publishing House.

Ohnuki-Tierney, E. 1980. "Ainu illness and healing: a symbolic interpretation." *Am. Ethnol.* 7: 132–51.

 1981. "Phases in human perception/conception/symbolization processes: cognitive anthropology and symbolic classification." *Am. Ethnol.* 8: 451–67.

Ong, A. 1987. *Spirits of Resistance and Capitalist Discipline*. New York, New York State University Press.

Oosten, J. G. 1980. *The Theoretical Structure of the Religion of the Netsilik and Iglulik*. Groningen, Meppel.

Opler, M. E. 1958. "Spirit possession in a rural area of northern India." In *Reader in Comparative Religion*, eds. W. A. Lessa and E. Z. Vogt. New York, Row, Peterson.

Opler, M. E., ed. 1959. *Culture and Mental Health*. New York, Macmillan.

Osinya, Alumidi. 1977. *Field Marshall Abdulla Salim Fisi (or How the Hyena Got His!)*. London, JOE Publications.

Packard, R. M. 1980. "Social change and the history of misfortune among the Bashu of Eastern Zaire." In *Explorations in African Systems of Thought*, eds. I. Karp and C. S. Bird. Bloomington, Indiana University Press.

Paques, Vivianne. 1964. *L'Arbre cosmique dans la pensée populaire et dans la vie quotidienne du nord-ouest africain*. Paris, Institut d'Ethnologie.

Parker, S. 1960. "The Wiitiko psychosis in the context of Ojibwa personality and culture." *American Anthropologist* 62: 603–23.

Parkin, D. 1970. "The politics of ritual syncretism: Islam among the non-Muslim Giriama of Kenya." *Africa* 40: 217–33.

    1972. *Palms, Wine and Witnesses*. London, Intertext Books.

Pearce-Higgins, J. D. 1957. *Resurrection: A Study of the Facts*. Worthing.

Penna, R. 1963. *La tarantella Napoletana*. Naples, Rivista di Etnografia.

Plowden, W. G. 1868. *Travels in Abyssinia and the Galla country*. London, Longmans Green.

Porter Poole, F. 1983. "Cannibals, tricksters and witches." In *The Ethnography of Cannibalism*, eds. P. Brown and D. Tuzin. Washington, D.C., Society for Psychological Anthropology.

Potapov, L. P. 1978. "Altic shamanism: an essay in historical dating." In *General Problems of Ethnography*, ed. S. A. Arutyonov. Moscow, Academy of Sciences, Institute of Ethnography.

Reichel-Dolmatoff, G. 1971. *Amazonian Cosmos*. Chicago, University of Chicago Press.

Reyna, S. P. 1994. "Literary anthropology and the case against science." *Man* 29, no. 3: 555–82.

Richards, A. 1967. "African systems of thought: an Anglo-French dialogue." *Man* 2, no. 2: 286–98.

    1968. "Keeping the king divine." *Proceedings Royal Anthropological Institute for 1968*: 23–36.

Rodinson, M. 1954. *Bibliotheca Orientalis*, xxi, 238–45.

Ross, C. 1989. *Multiple Personality Disorder*. New York, Wiley.

Rouch, J. 1960. *La religion et la magie Songhay*. Paris, Presses Universitaires de France.

Rouget, G. 1980. *La musique et la transe*. Paris, Gallimard.

Ruel, M. 1970. "Were-animals and the intraverted witch." In *Witchcraft Confessions and Accusations*, ed. M. Douglas. London, Tavistock Publications.

Sahlins, M. 1983. "Raw women, cooked men and other 'great things' of the Fiji Islands." In *The Ethnography of Cannibalism*, eds. P. Brown and D. Tuzin. Washington, D.C., Society for Psychological Anthropology.

Sanday, P. R. 1986. *Divine Hunger: Cannibalism as a Cultural System*. Cambridge, Cambridge University Press.

Sanjek, R., ed. 1990. *Fieldnotes: The Making of Anthropology*. Ithaca, Cornell University Press.

Saunders, L. W. 1977. "Variants in Zar experience in an Egyptian village." In *Case Studies in Possession*, eds. V. Crapanzano and V. Garrison. London, Wiley.

Schmidt, Pater W. 1912–54. *Der Ursprung der Gottesidee: eine historisch-kritische und positive Studie*. Munster, Aschendorffsche Verlagsbuchhandling.

Schnabel, J. 1995. *Dark White: Aliens, Abductions, and the UFO Obsession*. London, Hamish Hamilton.

Seymour-Smith, C. 1984. "Politics and ethnicity among the Peruvian Jivaro of the Rio communities." Unpublished Ph.D. thesis, University of London.

Shack, W. 1966. *The Gurage*. London, Oxford University Press.

Shepherd, M. 1981. *Psychiatric Illness in General Practice*. London, Oxford University Press.

Shepherd, M., Cooper, B., Brown, A. C. and Kalton, G. W. 1964. "Minor mental illness in London: some aspects of a general practice survey." *British Medical Journal* 2: 1359–63.

Shirokogoroff, S. M. 1935. *The Psychomental Complex of the Tungus*. London, Kegan Paul.

Siikala, A. L. 1978. *The Rite Technique of the Siberian Shaman*. Helsinki, FF Communications.

Siikala, A. L. and Hoppal, M. 1992. *Studies on Shamanism*. Budapest, Akademici Kiado.

Skinner, E. P. 1966. "Islam in Mossi society." In *Islam in Tropical Africa*, ed. I. M. Lewis. London, Oxford University Press.

Smith, M. G. 1957. "Social functions and meaning of Hausa praise-singing." *Africa* 27: 26–41.

    1962. "Exchange and marketing among the Hausa." In *Markets in Africa*, eds. P. Bohannan and G. Dalton. Evanston, Ill., Northwestern University Press.

Smith, Mary. 1954. *Baba of Karo*. London, Faber & Faber.

Sperber, D. 1976. "Dirt, danger and pangolins." *Times Literary Supplement*, April 30, 502–3.

Spiro, M. E. 1968. "Virgin birth, parthenogenesis and physiological paternity, an essay in cultural interpretation." *Man* 3, no. 2: 242–61.

    1978. *Burmese Supernaturalism*. New York, Prentice Hall, first edition 1967.

Stayt, H. 1931. *The BaVenda*. London, Oxford University Press.

Sternberg, L. 1924. "Divine election in primitive religion." *Proceedings of the 21st American Congress* 2: 472–512.

Stewart, K. 1946. "Spirit possession in native America." *South Western Journal of Anthropology* 2: 323–39.

Stocking, G. W., ed. 1983. *Observers Observed*. Madison, University of Wisconsin Press.

Strathern, A. 1982. "Witchcraft, greed, cannibalism and death: some related themes from the New Guinea Highlands." In *Death and the Regeneration of Life*, eds. M. Bloch and J. Parry. Cambridge, Cambridge University Press.

Strobel, M. 1979. *Muslim Women in Mombasa 1890–1975*. New Haven, Yale University Press.

Swantz, M. 1970. *Ritual and Symbol in Transitional Zaramo Society*. Uppsala, Gleerup.

ter Haar, G. and Ellis, S. 1988. "Spirit possession and healing in modern Zambia: an analysis of letters to Archbishop Milingo." *African Affairs* 87, no. 347: 185–206.

Thomas, K. 1971. *Religion and the Decline of Magic*. London, Allen Lane.

Thomas, N. and Humphrey, C., eds. 1994. *Shamanism, History and the State*. Ann Arbor, University of Michigan Press.

Thrupp, S. L., ed. 1962. *Millennial Dreams in Action*. The Hague, Mouton.

Tremearne, A. J. N. 1913. *Hausa Superstitions and Customs*. London, John Bale.

1914. *The Ban of the Bori: Demons and Demon-Dancing in West and North Africa*. London, Heath, Cranton & Ouseley.

Trimingham, J. S. 1959. *Islam in West Africa*. Oxford, Clarendon Press.

1968. *The Influence of Islam on Africa*. London, Longman.

Tubiana, J. 1954. "Un cult des genes agrestes en Ethiopie." *Rassegna di Studi Etiopici* 13: 76–90.

Tubiana, J. 1991. "*Zar* and *Buda* in northern Ethiopia." In *Women's Medicine*, eds. I. M. Lewis *et al.* Edinburgh, Edinburgh University Press.

Turner, R. 1970. "Witchcraft as negative charisma." *Ethnology* 9: 366–72.

Turner, V. W. 1960. "Muchona the hornet, interpreter of religion." In *In the Company of Man*, ed. J. B. Casagrande. New York, Harper.

1967. *The Forest of Symbols*. Ithaca, Cornell University Press.

1969. *The Ritual Process: Structure and Anti-Structure*. London, Routledge & Kegan Paul.

van Beek, W. E. A. 1991. "Dogon restudies: a field evaluation of the work of Marcel Griaule." *Current Anthropology* 32: 139–67.

Vansina, J. 1964. *Le royaume Kuba*. Tervuren.

Voigt, V. 1977. "Shamanism in Siberia." *Acta Ethnographica* 26: 385–95.

Wallace, A. F. C. 1959. "The institutionalization of cathartic and control strategies in Iroquois religious psychotherapy." In *Culture and Mental Health*, ed. M. K. Opler. New York, Macmillan.

1961. "Mental illness, biology and culture." In *Psychological Anthropology*, ed. F. L. K. Hsu. Homewood, Ill., Dorsey Press.

Watson, W. 1958. *Tribal Cohesion in a Money Economy*. Manchester, Manchester University Press.

Werbner, R. P. 1964. "Atonement ritual and guardian-spirit possession among the Kalanga." *Africa* 34: 206–22.

Werner, R. 1986. "Bomoh/Dukun: the practices and philosophies of the traditional Malay healer." *Studia Ethnologica Berniensia* 3.

Westermarck, E. A. 1926. *Ritual and Belief in Morocco*. (2 vols.) London, Macmillan.

Weyer, E. M. 1932. *The Eskimos: Their Environment and Folkways*. New Haven, Yale University Press.

Whisson, M. G. 1964. "Some aspects of functional disorders among the Kenya Luo." In *Magic, Faith and Healing*, ed. A. Kiev. New York, Free Press of Glencoe.

White, C. M. N. 1961. *Elements in Luvale Beliefs and Rituals*. (Rhodes-Livingstone Institute paper no. 32.) Lusaka, Rhodes-Livingstone Institute.

White, L. 1994. "'Firemen to not buy people': media, villains and vampires in Kampala in the 1950s." *Passages: a chronicle of the Humanities* 5, no. 1, issue 8: 11–17.

Whyte, S. R. 1981. "Men, women and misfortune in Bunyole." *Man* 16: 350–66.

Willis, R. 1975. *Man and beast*. London, Paladin.

Wilson, M. 1951. *Good Company: A study of Nyakyusa Age-Villages*. London, Oxford University Press.

Wilson, P. J. 1967. "Status ambiguity and spirit possession." *Man* 2 (n.s.), no. 3: 366–78.

1967. "Spirits and the sex war." *Man* 2 (n.s.), no. 4: 628–9.

Worsley, P. 1957. *The Trumpet Shall Sound: A Study of "Cargo" Cults in Melanesia*. London, MacGibbon & Kee.

Wyllie, R. W. 1973. "Introspective witchcraft among the Effutu of Southern Ghana." *Man* 8, no. 1: 74–9.

Young, A. 1975. "Why Amhara get *Kureynya*: sickness and possession in an Ethiopian *Zar* cult." *American Ethnologist* 2: 567–84.

Zaretsky, I. and Shambaugh, C. 1978. *Spirit Possession and Spirit Mediumship in Africa and Afro-America: An Annotated Bibliography.* New York, Garland Publishing.

Zuesse, E. M. 1979. *Ritual Cosmos.* Athens, GA, University of Ohio Press.

Index